Brodie James

Remarks on the Antiquity and Nature of Man

In Reply to the Recent Work of Charles Lyell

Brodie James

Remarks on the Antiquity and Nature of Man
In Reply to the Recent Work of Charles Lyell

ISBN/EAN: 9783337105013

Printed in Europe, USA, Canada, Australia, Japan

Cover: Foto ©Thomas Meinert / pixelio.de

More available books at **www.hansebooks.com**

REMARKS

ON THE

ANTIQUITY AND NATURE OF MAN,

IN

REPLY

TO THE

RECENT WORK OF SIR CHARLES LYELL.

BY THE
REV. JAMES BRODIE, A.M.

" Magna est veritas et prævalebit."

EDINBURGH:
JOHNSTONE, HUNTER, AND CO.
LONDON: HAMILTON, ADAMS, AND CO.
1864.

CONTENTS.

PREFACE.

In attempting to reply to the speculations contained in "Lyell's Antiquity of Man," the author of the following pages has endeavoured to state the arguments which Sir Charles employs, and the facts on which they rest, as clearly and as fairly as he possibly could, so that any one perusing the present publication may have the whole question fully before him.

He has not felt himself called on to notice disquisitions, however elaborate, which have no bearing either on the antiquity or on the nature of man, and he has seen no necessity for discussing facts which he was prepared to admit. All that he conceived to be required of him, was to specify the questions under debate, with the evidence brought forward on either side. His treatise, therefore, is brief, because the arguments adduced by Sir Charles, when separated from the mass of incongruous matter in which they are embedded, are but few in number, and do not require any lengthened discussion in order to enable an intelligent reader to form an opinion in regard to them.

Some will no doubt regard it as highly presumptuous in one who is utterly unknown to the world of science, to undertake a review of the work of an author so deservedly eminent; but when a man finds that which he believes to be THE TRUTH called into question, duty requires him at all hazards to maintain its cause, and to be no respecter of persons. And those who seek to be fully persuaded in their own minds, in reference to any subject that may be brought under their consideration, will not inquire, Who are the *advocates* by whom any particular opinion in regard to it is maintained? but, What are the *arguments* by which it is supported?

The author has only further to say, that any correction of his statements, or any suggestion tending to illustrate them, will be thankfully attended to.

MONIMAIL, CUPAR FIFE,
Feb. 17, 1864.

ANTIQUITY AND NATURE OF MAN.

INTRODUCTION.

AT the meeting of the British Association for the Advancement of Science, lately held at Newcastle, the work of Sir Charles Lyell on the Antiquity of Man, received such unqualified commendation from those who hold the highest rank .in the scientific world, that the words of the President, in his inaugural address, must be regarded as the decision of our modern philosophers :—" It seems no longer possible to doubt that the human race has existed on the earth, in a barbarian state, for a period far exceeding the limit of the historical record."

On the other hand, theologians of every denomination, who hold the Mosaic narrative to be the record of inspiration, believe that God made man perfect in mental powers and in bodily organization,—that the human ·race did not exist in a barbarian state for a period exceeding the limit of the historical record,— and that it is not yet six thousand years since they first appeared upon this sublunary sphere.

A

When science and theology are thus brought into seeming collision, it is the duty of every one who believes in God as at once the God of nature and the God of grace, to examine the subject with care, that he may devise a means by which this apparent discrepancy may be explained.

Some of those who devote themselves to philosophical pursuits, and at the same time profess regard for the sacred record, have suggested that, as the adoption of the conclusions to which geologists have come would not affect our belief in any of the essential doctrines of revelation, we should modify our views of the Hebrew chronology, in order to bring them into conformity with the discoveries of geologists.

To this proposal we cannot agree. We have examined, over and over again, the narrative of Moses, and the historical evidence adduced in its favour, and we feel fully persuaded, not only that it was at first a simple and accurate statement of facts, but that it has been brought down to us correct and unimpaired. We do not approve of the liberties which some translators have taken with the Hebrew text in their interpretations of its meaning; and we are prepared to maintain, that the plain and literal meaning of the words is perfectly consistent both with the doctrines of revelation and with the discoveries of science.

Another method of reconciliation is open before us. If the old Hebrew statements will not bend, the conclusions of modern geologists may be found more complying. We therefore turn to the volume of Sir C.

Lyell, that we may examine the facts which he has collected, and judge of the arguments which he has founded upon them.

In doing so, we find the solution of our difficulties made very easy. It needs only a very brief examination of his work to convince any careful, unprejudiced reader, that *a large proportion of the facts which he brings forward are not fairly stated, and that the conclusions to which he comes are not warranted by the evidence which he adduces.*

It is with great reluctance that we make such animadversions on any work of Sir C. Lyell. There is no writer of the present day whose publications we have read with greater pleasure. His vast stores of varied information, his shrewd observation in discovering facts, and his unwearied diligence in collecting them, entitle him to stand in the foremost rank of modern philosophers.

His eminence, however, in these respects, and the authority it imparts to his opinions, make it all the more to be regretted that, in framing hypotheses, he is deficient in that cautious examination of the evidence adduced, and that careful deduction of the conclusions to which it leads, without which we have no guarantee against error of the most extravagant kind. It is the high position which he holds as an author that gives to his arguments their currency and influence, and makes it imperative on those who hold a contrary opinion to point out the errors into which he has fallen.

The professed and primary object of his recent publication is to show that man has been a dweller upon earth for many thousand years. Its ultimate and special design, apparently, is to support Mr Darwin's theory of transmutation; in which it is affirmed that man, and all the other creatures found upon earth, have received their being through a slow process of adaptation, from a few simple organisms that existed in the early ages of our globe, and that man does not differ from the irrational animals in nature and essence, but only in degree of development.'

We shall endeavour to set the more important of his propositions, if we may so describe them, before our readers in as simple and intelligible a form as we can; though the manner in which his hypotheses, arguments, and facts are mixed up together is so confused, that it is no easy task to classify his observations, or to review his reasonings.

I.

THE TIME REQUIRED FOR THE UPHEAVAL OF RAISED BEACHES.

ONE of the evidences on which Sir Charles relies, as a proof of the great antiquity of man, is the length of time that must be supposed to have elapsed during the elevation of beds, in which the relics of human art are mixed with shells and other marine remains. We shall give his argument in his own words :—

"It has long been a fact familiar to geologists, that, both on the east and west coasts of the central part of Scotland there are lines of raised beaches, containing marine shells of the same species as those now inhabiting the neighbouring sea. The two most marked of these littoral deposits occur at heights of about forty and twenty-five feet above high-water mark. . . . . . In those districts where large rivers, such as the Clyde, the Forth, and the Tay, enter the sea, the lower of the two deposits, or that of twenty-five feet, expands into a terrace fringing the estuary, and varying in breadth from a few yards to several miles. Of this nature are the flat lands which occur along the margin of the Clyde at Glasgow, out of which, previous to the year 1858, no less than seventeen canoes had been dug. Nearly all of these ancient boats were formed out of a single oak stem, hollowed out by blunt tools, probably stone axes, aided by the action of fire. A few were cut beautifully smooth, evidently with metallic tools. One, dug up at Bankton, was eighteen feet

in length, and very elaborately constructed. . . . . . There
can be no doubt that some of these buried vessels are of far
more ancient date than the others. . . . . . The regularly
built boat at Bankton may perhaps have come within the age of
iron.

" Recent explorations, by Mr Geikie and Dr Young, of the
sites of old Roman harbours, along the southern margin of the
Frith of Forth, lead to similar inferences. Inveresk is the site
of an ancient Roman port; and if we suppose the sea to have
washed the foot of the heights on which the town stood, the tide
would have ascended far up the Valley of the Esk, and would
have made the mouth of that river a safe and commodious harbour; whereas, had it been a shoaling estuary, as at present, it
is difficult to see how the Romans should have made choice of
it as a port.

" At Cramond was Alaterva, the chief Roman harbour on the
south-west of the Forth, where numerous coins, urns, and sculp-
tured stones, and the remnant of a harbour, have been detected.
The old Roman quays, built along what must have been the sea
margin, have been found on what is now dry ground, with a
dreary expanse of mud extending outward well-nigh two miles.
Had these shoals existed eighteen centuries ago, they would
have prevented the Romans from making this a port; whereas,
if the land were now to sink twenty feet, Cramond would
unquestionably be the best natural harbour along the whole of
the south side of the Forth. . . . .

" There seems strong presumption in favour of the opinion,
that the date of the elevation may have been subsequent to the
Roman occupation.

" But the twenty-five feet rise is only the last stage of a long
antecedent process of elevation; for examples of recent marine
shells have been observed forty feet and upwards above the sea
in Argyleshire. At one of these localities a rude ornament of
cannel coal has been found, fifty feet above the sea level, covered
with gravel containing marine shells.

" If we suppose the upward movement to have been uniform

in central Scotland, before and after the Roman era. and assume that as twenty-five feet indicates seventeen centuries, so fifty feet imply a lapse of twice that number, or three thousand four hundred years, we should then carry back the date of the ornament in question to fifteen centuries before our era, or to the period usually assigned to the exodus of the Israelites from Egypt." (Pp. 47, 48, &c.)

There is another movement, an "argument from Scandinavia," as Professor Phillips termed it, at the recent meeting of the British Association, to which Sir Charles more frequently refers. We again quote his own statements :—

"The upward movement now in progress, in parts of Norway and Sweden, extends throughout an area of a thousand miles north and south, and for an unknown distance east and west, the amount of elevation always increasing as we proceed towards the North Cape, where it is said to equal five feet in a century. If we could assume that there had been an average rise of two and a-half feet in each hundred years for the last fifty centuries, this would give an elevation of one hundred and twenty-five feet in that period. A mean rate of continuous vertical elevation of two and a-half feet in a century would, I conceive, be a high average." (P. 58.)

Let us now see how he applies the rule he thus forms :—

"Count Albert de la Marmora, in his description of the geology of Sardinia, has shown that, on the southern coast of that island, at Cagliari and in the neighbourhood, an ancient bed of the sea, containing marine shells of living species, and numerous fragments of antique pottery, has been elevated from seventy to ninety-eight metres above the present level of the Mediterranean. Oysters and other shells, many of them having

both valves united, occur embedded in a breccia, in which fragments of limestone abound. Besides pieces of coarse pottery, a
flattened ball of baked earthenware, with a hole through its
axis, was found in the midst of marine shells. It is supposed
to have been used for weighting a fishing net. If we assume
the average rate of upheaval to have been as before hinted (p.
58), two and a-half feet in a century, three hundred feet would
give an antiquity of twelve thousand years to the Cagliari
pottery, even if we simply confine our estimate to the upheaval
above the sea level, without allowing for the original depth of
water in which the mollusca lived." (P. 178.)

Similar arguments are employed in regard to the
elevation of the valley of the Somme, to which more
particular attention will afterwards be directed.

To these statements we oppose the following objections :—1. He takes no notice of the fact, that the
action of the billows produces a high-water as well as
a low-water terrace. 2. He speaks of the rise of these
beaches as continuous, whereas the level surface which
they exhibit is itself an evidence of sudden upheaval.
3. He assumes the rising of the land in Sweden to be
the measure by which we are to calculate the action
of internal agencies in other places, although it is well
known that no general measure can be assigned.

In order to substantiate the first of these objections,
we must direct our attention to the nature of that mechanical action of the water by which those level
beaches or terraces are formed.

When we look on the sea in a storm, and see it
dashing its breakers against the shore, we are tempted
to imagine that the ocean must be moved to its lowest

depths. This, however, is far from being the case. It is only a few feet of the surface water that is affected by the tempest. One or two fathoms down, the watery mass is either altogether still, or glides along in gentle flow. Keeping this in mind, let us trace the course of a pebble lying on the beach. When the waves strike against the shore, the pebble is hurried upwards towards the land; but when the billows again retreat, it is carried back. This process is repeated again and again. If the retreating wave prove the stronger, the stone is carried farther and farther back, till at last it reaches a depth where the agitation of the surface can no longer disturb its repose. Other pieces of stone and shell are in like manner brought down, and laid beside the first, and others again are carried still farther into the deep, rolling over the former ones, and resting behind them. In this manner a submarine terrace, or level, is formed. Its depth, under low-water mark, will depend upon the size of the waves and other modifying circumstances. When currents prevail, as is usually the case on the coasts of an open sea, the deposit thus formed will be spread irregularly over the bottom. In friths and land-locked creeks it will be comparatively level.

If by any convulsion of nature the relative height of the sea and land be altered, so that the terrace formed under the low-water mark is raised above the influence of the high-water billow, there will then be a tract of level land gained from the sea, on which water-worn pebbles and marine remains will be found,

affording abundant evidence of the change that has
taken place. The remains of the ancient canoes found
in the neighbourhood of Glasgow are sufficient proof
that the level ground on the banks of the Clyde were
formed in this manner. They evidently owe their
preservation to their submergence under the waves.
If they had not been protected from atmospheric influence, by the muddy sediment in which. they were
embedded, they would very speedily have rotted away
and left no trace behind. The Carse of Stirling, and
a large proportion of the raised beaches that are found
on the coast of Scotland, appear to have been formed
in the same way.

While, however, we look to this deposition of sedi-
mentary matter under low-water mark as the means
by which the larger part of these raised beaches have
been originally formed, we must not forget that the
action of the waves produces another level, or terrace, of a different kind. Every observer, who has
walked along the sea-shore, must have remarked that
while many substances, swept backwards and forwards
by the tide, are gradually carried into the deep, others
are thrown up on the beach and there left dry. The
material thus cast up, of whatever kind it may be, does
not find a final resting-place till it has been carried
up beyond the reach of the water at the highest flood.
When the land is advancing on the sea, and the quantity of *debris* swept along by the tide is large, the
gravel, sea-weed, and shells, thus thrown up, form a
bank or terrace, which varies in height above high-

water mark, according to the strength of the wave. Such banks, from ten to twenty feet above ordinary tide mark, and of considerable extent, are sometimes formed. These upper terraces, as we may call them, are exposed to the influence of the weather, and to the effects of succeeding tides and storms, and, consequently, are irregular in their levels, and are seldom continuous for any great extent along the shore. They sometimes consist of shingle, and sometimes of sand. Instances of such terraces may be found in many places all along the British coasts. A large proportion of what are called " downs " in England, and " links " in Scotland, seem to have been thrown up in this manner.

Two terraces are thus formed,—a lower one, from five to fifteen feet below low-water mark, and an upper one, from five to fifteen feet above ordinary high-water level. Allowing fifteen feet for the rise and fall of the tide, the one of these terraces will be from twenty-five to forty or fifty feet higher than the other.

When Sir Charles, therefore, tells us of some beaches that are raised twenty-five feet above the present high-water level, and of others that are from forty to fifty feet above it, we are naturally led to suppose, that these beaches were not successive formations, separated from each other by long intervening ages, but that they were produced by the action of the waves, in different circumstances, during the same period of time. There is no reason why we should not consider the cannel coal ornament, on which Sir Charles places so much reliance, as contemporaneous with the canoes found on the banks of the Clyde.

We may remark in passing, that we find inaccuracies in Sir Charles's statements, the correction of which would render his conclusions of little value, even if we were to adopt his own hypothesis.

He says that there is strong presumption for the opinion, that the upheaval of the central portion of Scotland took place after the Roman era, and then he speaks of the seventeen centuries which have elapsed since the event occurred. The Romans began their invasion of Scotland in A.D. 80. In A.D. 209 their dominion was extended farther over the country than at any previous period. And they finally left it in A.D. 420. The date of the upheaval, according to his own estimate, therefore, cannot have been more than fifteen centuries ago.

There is another, and more important inaccuracy. The Carse of Stirling and the Valley of Clyde bear evident marks of having been formed in the still water under low-water mark, and consequently, as we have shown, from twenty to twenty-five feet below high-water mark. If they are now twenty-five feet above it, the total elevation has been at least forty-five feet. Even on the supposition, therefore, that the rise has been gradual, the date of the upheaval of the fifty feet beach, in which the cannel coal ornament was found, would only be five or six hundred years before Christ,—the era of the Babylonish captivity, and not that of the exodus from Egypt, as Sir Charles supposes.

We stated, as a second objection to Sir Charles's conclusions, that he speaks of the rises of these beaches as continuous, whereas the level surface which they exhibit is itself an evidence of sudden upheaval. When we examine these deposits, we find them, without exception, of such incoherent material, that if they had been subjected to the action of the billows during a slow and gradual elevation, they must have been washed away. The muddy loam of the Carse, and the loose gravel of the twenty-five feet beach, could not have resisted the action of the sea. Nothing but their sudden elevation could have preserved the horizontal form. A gradual rise would not produce a level terrace, but a sloping bank.

Our principal objection, however, to his argument is, that he assumes the rising of the land in Sweden to be the measure by which we are to calculate the action of internal agencies in other places. He speaks of a continuous rise in Sweden; but he makes no mention of the many sudden changes of level that have taken place in various parts of the world, both in ancient and modern times. If all the evidence in regard to the elevation and depression of the land was fully investigated, we are very much inclined to suspect that sudden upheaval would be found to be the rule, and continuous elevation the exception. We therefore object to his reasoning, and maintain that this bringing forward of one class of facts, while others of a different kind are passed by in silence, gives an unfair and one-sided view of the question. There is

not the shadow of evidence for concluding that the
elevation of those beaches was slow and continuous.

As to the changes in Italy, we have no reason to
conclude that they have been uniformly progressive;
and even if we were to allow that the elevation of
Cagliari was gradual, there is no ground for assuming
that the rate was two and a-half feet in a century.
If the North Cape is rising at the rate of five feet in
a hundred years, may not the southern part of Sardinia have risen with equal rapidity? We again ask,
Why are we to take the elevation of Sweden as the
rule to measure the rate of upheaval in Italy? The
region in which Cagliari is situated is altogether
different from that which is occupied by Scandinavia.
In the one there are three volcanoes—Vesuvius, Etna,
and Stromboli,—all in active operation, while earthquakes and sudden convulsions of nature are of frequent occurrence. In the other there is no volcano,
and earthquakes, we believe, are rare. If we are to
speculate on the time required for the elevation of
Cagliari, let us take our example of a rise from some
of the neighbouring shores. In 1538 the whole
coast of Puzzuoli, near Naples, was raised twenty feet
in a single night. If, therefore, taking this fact as
the basis of our calculations, we were to conclude that
it took fifteen days to raise the southern part of Sardinia, we would have far better ground on which to
rest our argument than the arbitrary assumption of
Sir Charles.

In truth, however, all speculations as to the time

required by internal agency for accomplishing the most startling results are simply absurd. The elevation of a mountain, or the hollowing out of a sea, may result from changes slowly progressing during many, many centuries; or they may be effected by subterranean forces in a single hour.

II.

THE TIME REQUIRED FOR THE CHANGE OF CLIMATE AND EXTINCTION OF SPECIES.

THE argument on which the conclusions of modern geologists, in reference to the antiquity of man, more especially depend, is the length of time that must be supposed to have elapsed in order to effect a change of climate, like that which seems to have taken place in the western part of Europe since man became an inhabitant there, and to allow for the extinction of various species of mammalia, with which he appears to have been contemporary in the earlier stages of his existence.

We shall not attempt to controvert their statements as to facts, though, it may be, we are not always without some misgivings as to the accuracy of their observations and the impartiality of the descriptions. It is the province of the practical geologist to collect and prepare the information, and with that department we do not intermeddle. As, however, every one is at liberty to judge for himself as to the value of the arguments that are founded upon the information laid before him, and as to the soundness of the conclusions to which they lead, we shall take the liberty of calling in question their conjectures and speculations, and do not feel that it is a very presumptuous undertaking that we attempt, inasmuch as a very moderate acquaintance with the elements of mechanical philosophy is all that is requisite for the task.

After the Tertiary epochs had passed away, a period ensued when the whole of the western part of Europe was depressed from one to two thousand feet below its present level, so that the tops of our mountains formed islands in the midst of the sea. At the same time intense cold prevailed, and these islands were not only subjected to the influence of icebergs floating past them, but were themselves " centres of glacial action." Huge masses of ice were formed upon them, which far exceeded in size any glacier now existing in Europe. This ice moving slowly downward, as glaciers are found to do, swept before it all the loose material , lying on the surface of the ground, and gradually wore down the rocks themselves, and covered the valleys around with their disintegrated remains. The deposit produced by these means differs in its composition, according to the nature of the rock from which it is derived. It consists of what was at one time mud, with which are intermingled sand, and gravel, and boulders of stone. It constitutes the "loess" of the Continent, and the "boulder clay" of Britain. Of this period Sir Charles gives a long and particular account.

. After this "glacial epoch" had passed, Europe seems to have been elevated to within fifty or a

hundred feet of its present level. It was then ten-
anted by plants and animals similar to those which it
now supports. Among the animals, however, a good
many were found that are now extinct, at least in the
districts which they then inhabited—as for instance,
elephants, rhinoceroses, lions, bears, reindeer, and elks.
This period Sir Charles has named the Post-Pliocene.
In the earlier portion of it the extinct mammalia seem
to have predominated; and the number of their remains that have been discovered, show that the duration of the era in which they lived must have been
very great. The reindeer and fossil elephant are
known to have been formed for living in arctic regions. It has, therefore, been supposed, that the
climate of the middle, and perhaps, also, of the south
of Europe, during that epoch, resembled that which is
at present found in the northern parts of Sweden and
Russia. There are other considerations which make
this supposition highly probable.

During the latter part of this Post-Pliocene period,
there is reason to conclude that man was an inhabitant
of Europe. In caves, through which streams of water
seem to have flowed, the remains of the human skeleton have been found, along with bones of animals now
extinct. There, also, are found implements of flint,
and all so intermingled, as to show that they must
have been contemporary. In fact, the position of
these remains suggests the idea, that, instead of in-
terring their dead, the aborigines of Europe committed
their deceased companions to these watery caverns,

with their weapons of the chase in their hands, and a portion of their prey beside them.↗ In beds of gravel, of considerable depth, these bones are found along with implements of flint. In one instance an ancient burial place was discovered, containing a number of human skeletons, and beside it the remains of what are supposed to have been funeral feasts in honour of the dead. Among the ashes were found bones of animals now extinct, the flesh of which had formed the repast. That man was contemporary with these creatures, therefore, does not seem to admit of a doubt.

At an after time the land appears to have been raised to its present position, that is, from fifty to a hundred feet above its former level. There are also traces of movements by which rocks have been rent asunder, valleys laid open, and the courses of rivers changed. The climate also was ameliorated, and the gigantic mammalia disappeared. This constitutes what Sir Charles calls the Recent Period.

Sir Charles argues that, since man has been a dweller on earth in the Post-Pliocene as well as in the Recent Period, he must have come into this sublunary sphere many thousand years ago :—

"When we desire to reason or speculate on the probable antiquity of human bones found fossil in such situations as the caverns near Liege, there are two classes of evidence to which we may appeal for our guidance :—First, considerations of the time required to allow of many species of carnivorous and herbivorous animals, which flourished in the cave period, becoming first scarce, and then so entirely extinct, as we have seen that they became before the era of the Danish peat and Swiss lake dwellings. Secondly, the great number of centuries necessary for the conversion of the physical geography of the Liege district from its ancient to its present configuration; so many old underground channels, through which brooks and rivers flowed in the cave period, being now laid dry and choked up." (P. 73.)

We find in this reasoning what seems to us to be one of the strangest of fallacies. He describes great effects, and then he speaks of "considerations of time," but does not so much as allude to the forces that produced the effects. Every mechanician knows, that if the force or producing cause be known, we then can calculate the time required to accomplish a given result; but if the cause be unknown, it is perfectly idle to speculate as to the question of time. One of the primary elements on which our calculation must rest is awanting.

' Sir Charles assumes that the effects referred to were produced by some slowly operating cause; but though he speaks of " evidence to which we may appeal," he brings forward no evidence whatever in support of his conjecture.

As to the considerations of time required to allow many species of animals to become first scarce and then extinct, we reply, that though time kills the individuals, it does not kill the race. If the physical condition of the country had been unaltered, if no unwonted disease, and no new cause of death had appeared, the fossil elephant, the cave bear, and their early associates, had been still alive. The cause of their extinction must be sought in some change affecting the district in which they lived, the occurrence of some dire epidemic, or the arrival of some new and formidable assailant.

In regard to the changes of the physical geography of the country, we remark that these changes, in so far as we can follow the description given of them, have a very close resemblance to the effects produced by volcanic convulsions ; and we find it stated (p. 74), that "it is more than probable that the rate of change was once far more active than it is now," and that volcanic influence "may have been connected and co-eval with repeated risings and sinkings in the basin of the Meuse;" and though Sir Charles assumes the slow, continuous rise of the land in Sweden as the measure that should generally be adopted, we refer to the state-ments which we made before, as affording sufficient reason for concluding, that subterraneous influence does not in general act slowly and continuously ; and therefore, centuries are not required to account for the changes referred to.

It is sufficient for our argument to show that Sir Charles's considerations as to time rest on a basis alto-gether inadequate for their support. We shall, how-ever, adduce a conjectural, yet highly probable cause, to which all the changes referred to may be assigned.

The western parts of Europe, and more particularly the British Isles, enjoy an average temperature higher by many degrees than that which prevails in other countries under similar parallels of latitude. This peculiarity is ascribed, and with evident reason, to the

effects of what is usually termed the Gulf Stream.
The waters of the Atlantic, after they have been heated
in the Gulf of Mexico, and other intertropical parts of
the ocean, flow northward along the coast of America,
forming a well-known and very remarkable current.
This current, when it strikes against Newfoundland
and the great bank that adjoins that island, is deflected
eastward towards our shores, and communicates to us
a warmth that would otherwise have been unknown.
If that island and its great bank were sunk an hundred
fathoms below the present level, the Gulf Stream
would pass up through Davis' Straits into the Polar
Sea, and expend its genial influence on the northern
archipelago.   At the same time, the returning current
of cold water from the pole, which now comes down
through the straits, would flow along the coasts of
Europe, and, freighted with islands of floating ice,
would reduce the' temperature of our climate as far below the average warmth of corresponding latitudes as
it is now above it.

    This seems to have been the cause of the cold that
prevailed in Europe during the glacial period.   At that
time Scotland was submerged two thousand feet below
the deep; other parts of Europe shared in the depression; and we have only to suppose that a corresponding
change took place in the north-eastern shores of America, to find a cause which seems abundantly adequate
to explain the phenomena of that remarkable time.

    When that rise of the land which marked the com-
mencement of the Post-Pliocene, or Mammoth era, took

place, we may suppose that a similar elevation occurred in America. In that case the Gulf Stream would be divided—part of its influence being expended on America, and part on Europe; and the climate of western Europe would be, as it were, a medium between the temperature of the glacial and that of the present era.

A further upheaval of the American coast, similar to that which is generally allowed to have taken place on our own shores, would explain the increased warmth of the Recent Period.

If this conjecture be admitted, and there is nothing improbable in it, we have an intelligible and sufficient reason assigned for the destruction of " many species of carnivorous and herbivorous animals which flourished in the cave period." They seem to have been fitted for living in an arctic clime. A succession of ages would not have thinned their numbers, if the physical condition of the country had remained unchanged; but the introduction of an enervating climate, which might either induce disease, or render them weak and inactive, combined with the destructive weapons of a daring and intelligent adversary, would speedily sweep them away.

The change we refer to may have taken place in a single season, and it may not be more than three thousand years since the aborigines of Britain hunted the mammoth and rhinoceros, and, finding them enfeebled by the unwonted warmth of the air, made them an easy prey.

Though man may have been coeval with animals now extinct, and though changes in the climate, as well as in the physical geography of Europe, may have taken place since he first visited its shores, these circumstances do not prove him to have been an inhabitant of the earth for many thousand years.

III.

THE TIME REQUIRED FOR THE DEPOSITION AND REMOVAL OF GRAVEL BEDS.

IN a good many instances the remains of human art have been found in beds of gravel, from ten to twenty feet deep. They are frequently intermingled with the bones of extinct mammalia. Some portions of the human skeleton have been discovered in similar positions.

The most remarkable of these discoveries are those which have been made in the valley of the Somme, in Picardy. As they are usually regarded as affording evidence strongly confirmatory of Sir Charles's theory, we shall endeavour to give such an abridgment of his account as. may set the leading facts of the case distinctly before our readers.

The valley is hollowed out of a region of white chalk intermingled with flints. The banks which border the valley are between two and three hundred feet in height. After reaching that elevation, we find an extensive table-land, with gentle undulations, in which the chalk is covered with loam about five feet thick, forming a soil of great fertility. The valley is about a mile in average width. At Abbeville, twenty miles from the mouth of the river, " if thirty feet of peat were now removed, the sea would flow up and fill the valley for miles above that place." At Amiens, thirty miles farther up the valley, the Somme is about fifty feet above the sea.

We have a section given us of the valley, from which it appears that, in the bottom, immediately above the chalk, there is first a bed of gravel from three to fourteen feet in thickness; above that, there lies a bed of peat, from ten to thirty feet in thickness, lying on either side of the present channel of the Somme. At the sides of the valley, lying on the sloping chalk, are beds of gravel. The first is usually known by the name of the " lower level gravel," and is from twenty to forty feet thick; the second is the " upper level gravel," thirty feet in thickness.

The peat is of comparatively recent date; and any remains that have been found in it are those of animals belonging to species still alive. The lower level gravel contains many bones of animals of which the species are now extinct. Some of these bones are rounded, as if they had been rolled in running water; some are broken, and others are neither broken nor rounded, and seem as if they had been articulated together when they were covered up. Along with them, in several places, are found a great many implements made of flint. Some of these implements are of a spear-headed form, and vary in length from six to eight inches; others are of an oval shape, not unlike the stone implements used by the natives of Australia, and from five to six inches in length. Another variety consists of splinters, apparently intended for knives or arrow heads; they are about three inches in length. All these tools have been brought into shape by striking chips or splinters from the edge of the piece of flint out of which they were made. There are also a number of very rude implements, many of which may have been rejected as failures, and others struck off in the course of manufacturing the more perfect ones. The valley of the Somme, in short, seems to have been the Sheffield or Birmingham of those early times, to which the aborigines of Gaul resorted for the manufacture of their weapons. Some of these implements have their edges more or less fractured, either by use as instruments before they were buried in the gravel, or by being rolled in the river's bed.

The upper level gravel contains the same fossils as the lower. The section represents the lower level as forming a narrow terrace on both sides of the valley; the upper level appears on one side only.

Both in the upper and lower beds, pieces of stone are found which have all their edges and corners entire; this suggests the idea of their having been floated down by means of ice, so that they escaped the friction to which they would have been subjected if rolled along the bottom of the river. There are also contortions of the strata of sand and gravel, such as are caused by masses of ice brought down by a stream; these are most conspicuous in the upper beds.

Sir Charles tells us, that it has been a matter of

discussion, whether the higher or the lower levels are the more ancient. He holds the opinion, that the upper formations are the older ones, and that the period of their deposition was separated from that of the lower by a vast interval of time, while the scooping out of the valley, after the formation of the lower level, occupied a still more lengthened space.

" The peat of the valley of the Somme is a formation which, in all likelihood, took thousands of years for its growth. But no change of a marked character has occurred in the mammalian fauna since it began to accumulate. Hence, we may infer that the interval of time which separated the era of the large extinct mammalia from that of the earliest peat, was of far longer duration than that of the entire growth of the peat. Yet we by no means need the evidence of the ancient fossil fauna to establish the antiquity of man in this part of France. The mere volume of the drift, at various heights, would alone suffice to demonstrate a vast lapse of time during which such heaps of shingle, derived both from the Eocene and the Cretaceous rocks, were thrown down in a succession of river channels." (P. 144.)

" If the Menchecourt beds, near Abbeville, had been first formed, and the valley, after being nearly as deep and wide as it is now, had subsided, the sea must have advanced inland, causing small delta-like accumulations at successive heights, wherever the main river and its tributaries met the sea. Such a movement, especially if it were intermittent, and interrupted occasionally by long pauses, would very well account for the accumulation of stratified debris which we encounter at certain points in the valley, especially around Abbeville and Amiens. But we are precluded from adopting this theory by the entire absence of marine shells, and the presence of fresh water and land species, and mammalian bones, in considerable abundance, in the drift both of higher and lower levels above Abbeville." (P. 131.)

According to the hypothesis here suggested, the valley of the Somme, scooped out of the chalk at some previous epoch, had by some means unknown been filled with debris of the surrounding rocks, so that, at the time when the present formations began, the stream flowed along the upper level gravel. Sir Charles then supposes that the river currents swept out the hollow to the depth of the lower level gravel, and afterwards scooped it out still farther down to the gravel underlying the peat.

This supposition seems to us to be altogether untenable. Our present inquiry does not lead us to ask by what means the valley was originally scooped out of the chalk, and we shall take it for granted, that at the time when, according to Sir Charles's theory, the river ran along the high level terrace, the valley up to that height was filled with gravel. But we maintain that the agent he supposes could never have produced the effects which he assigns to it. The Somme drains but a limited district of country, and could never have brought down a great volume of water. The fall between Amiens and Abbeville is only two feet in a mile, and it would seem that the descent between Abbeville and the sea is still more gentle. Such a river might be imagined, in the course of some vastly extended period, to have filled up the valley with fine sand and mud; but it could not possibly have cleared out the gravel with which Sir Charles supposes it to have been filled. Some other and more powerful instrumentality must have been employed.

The appearances which the valley presents suggest to our minds the effects which we expect to find in a narrow estuary, or river influenced by the tide. ˙ Let us suppose that the valley shared in the depression, of which we see so many evidences in other districts, and that it was sunk a hundred feet below its present level. If we understand aright the description given of them, the lower level gravel would then be from five to ten feet below low-water mark, and the upper level gravel from five to ten feet above high-water mark. Between Abbeville and the ocean there would be an estuary, too narrow and too shallow to admit of the entrance of currents from the ocean, excepting near the mouth, and consequently filled with fresh water, and containing only fluviatile and terrestrial deposits. It would, however, be affected by the tides. The " absence of marine deposits " does not prove that the mechanical influence of the tidal flux and reflux was excluded. Between Abbeville and Amiens there would be a continuation of this narrow basin, becoming gradually shallower as it receded from the sea. In such a case, the force of the ascending and descending tide, like that now seen in the Solway Frith, would be very great. If we further keep in mind that, in the Post-Pliocene epoch, the winters must have been much more severe than they are now, and that there must have been large masses of ice formed in the estuary itself, besides those brought down by the Somme, we can easily perceive that these blocks, as they were swept up and down by the tide, must have acted with prodigious force on the sides of the basin.

Sir Charles's description represents the upper gravel as being thirty feet above the lower one. We formerly showed that this is the distance we may expect to find between the high-water and low-water terraces, formed by the ordinary action of the tide. If the Somme formerly brought down large quantities of floating ice, as we are led to suppose was the case, we may conclude that the spring and winter floods must have torn away large portions of its banks, whether they were formed of gravel or of chalk. The quantity of rubbish brought down by the stream would consequently be great, and, added to the sand and gravel abraded from the sides of the valley by the action of the tide and floating ice, would afford abundant mate-rial for a high-water terrace. On this terrace, moreover, the floating ice would most commonly be thrown, with the sand and stones adhering to it. Sir Charles's section represents the upper gravel as found only on one side of the valley, which seems to show that, like the high-water terraces on our own shores, it was not continuous. We are therefore led to conclude, that the upper and lower level gravels of the Somme may have been formed like the terraces we see in the creeks and estuaries of the British coasts, and consequently are to be regarded as contemporaneous.

Even, however, if this supposition should prove inadmissible, and we were to allow that the upper level gravel was formed in the same manner as the

lower, and deposited at an earlier date, we are not
necessitated to believe that " a vast distance of time "
separated their origin. If we admit the supposition
that, at the time the lower level was formed, the
valley of the Somme was a basin of water influenced
by the tidal wave, the upper gravel must have been
only some ten feet above high-water mark, and, consisting of a loose and incoherent mass, could not long
resist the action of the billows, excepting in those
places where, in some way or other, it was protected
from their force. It would not require " thousands of
years " to wash its contents down to the lower level :
a very few seasons would be amply sufficient.

As for the time required for the scooping out of
the valley, after the levels were formed, the "scour"
of the tide, the force of its flux and reflux, would
speedily remove beds of sand and gravel. We incline
to think, moreover, that we have no reason for supposing that any such scooping was necessary, or that the
gravels extended to any great distance beyond the
space which they now occupy. When Sir Charles
describes the parallel roads in Glen Roy, he tells us
that " there is one point on which all are agreed,
namely, that the shelves found there are ancient
beaches, accumulated around the edges of one or more
sheets of water, which once stood for a long time successively at the level of the different shelves." No
one has ever imagined that Glen Roy was first filled
up with gravel to a level with these roads, and then
hollowed out ; and there is no reason why it should be

considered necessary to allow ages for the reopening of the valley of the Somme.

The hypothesis of Sir Charles Lyell, even if we receive without questioning all his suppositions, seems to us untenable, inasmuch as it assumes an agency which could not, in any conceivable amount of time, have produced the effects which he assigns to it. The hypothesis which we have ventured to suggest, and which only assumes that the valley of the Somme has undergone an elevation similar to that which is known to have been experienced in other districts, both in Britain and on the Continent, implies the presence of a force which we see daily in operation, and which is amply sufficient, in the course of a few centuries, to produce results even greater than those of which we find evidence in the upper and lower level gravels.

All that the discoveries hitherto made can fairly be regarded as proving, amounts only to this—that for some time before the climate of Europe attained to its present anomalous mildness, and while some of the gigantic mammalia were still alive, the rude aborigines of Gaul came to the banks of the Somme to collect flints for the manufacture of their weapons of hunting and war. There is, however, no reason for assigning to these events a very remote antiquity. If the hypothesis which we have adduced be even possible,—and we maintain that it is not only a possible but a highly probable explanation of the appearances described,—we say here, as we said before, that it may not be more than three thousand years since man carried on his

c

exterminating war against the mammoth and its con-
temporaries.

FLINT IMPLEMENTS IN ENGLAND.

There are different places in England, more particularly near the eastern coast, where implements of
flint have been found in beds of gravel.

In some cases these implements are so intermingled
with the remains of the Post-Pliocene mammalia,
that we are led to conclude that, at least for a time,
man must have been coeval with the mammoth and
his congeners. To the argument in support of the
antiquity of man derived from this intermingling of
articles formed by human art with the remains of animals which are now extinct, we have already replied,
and need not again refer to it.

In several instances the thickness of the gravel
that overlies the relics of a prehistoric age is very considerable, and affords evidence, that since the period
of their manufacture very great changes must have
occurred in the localities where these discoveries have
been made. It has, therefore, been alleged, that the
fabrication of these implements must be referred to a
very ancient period. We remark, however, that the
time required for the deposition of gravel beds must
depend on the nature of the agency by which they
are produced, and that we can come to no conclusion
on the subject, unless we, in the first place, ascertain
what that agency was.

In the instances now under consideration this is attended with some difficulty. We are not ourselves acquainted with the districts in which these manufactures of the olden time have been found, and the description given by Sir Charles Lyell does not afford sufficient data for a precise determination of the question. It is evident, however, that the rivers and brooks, by the sides of which the deposits are found, if they were no larger in former times than they are now, could not possibly have effected the changes that the gravel beds have undergone. We may, indeed, affirm, that these beds cannot have been produced by the action of river floods of any kind, unless we suppose that some vast stream rose in an elevated district which lay to the west and south of England, in a locality now sunk beneath the waves of the Atlantic, and, after rolling its torrents over the middle of the country, fell into the German Ocean, near the place where we now find the mouths of the Nen and the Ouse. This supposition is so destitute of probability that it cannot be entertained.

There is another cause to which the changes in these gravel beds may be assigned. They may have been produced by the action of the tide in shallow estuaries. Of such action we have examples in many places; and we know that it is sufficiently powerful in its operation to afford a satisfactory explanation of the appearances that are exhibited. This hypothesis would only require us to suppose that England, in the Post-Pliocene epoch, was sunk below its present level to

a depth of from fifty to a hundred feet; and various
considerations render this supposition by no means
improbable.

If this theory be admitted as affording the probable,
or even the possible explanation of the appearances
exhibited, we need not engage in any debate as to the
period when these changes took place.   To all the arguments in favour of the antiquity of man, which are
derived from the discovery of implements of flint in
English gravel beds, we reply, as we did to those
deduced from the discoveries that have been made in
the valley of the Somme:—the beds of gravel cannot be
ascribed to the effects of river floods; they have in all
probability been produced by the action of the tide;
and that agency is at once so powerful, and so uncer-
tain and irregular in its operation, that it is idle to
speculate on the time which it required to effect the
changes which these localities have undergone.

IV.

THE MECHANICAL EFFECTS OF A FLOOD.

IN no case do the opinions of Sir Charles Lyell appear to us so far in error as when he speaks of the effects produced by a flood.

In page 192 he gives the following description of the volcanic cones of Auvergne:—

"We behold in many a valley of Auvergne, within fifty feet of the present river channel, a volcanic cone of loose ashes, with a crater at its summit, from which powerful currents of basaltic lava have poured, usurping the ancient bed of the torrent. By the action of the stream, in the course of ages, vast masses of the hard columnar basalt have been removed, pillar after pillar, and much vesicular lava, as in the case, for example, of the Puy Rouge, near Chalucet, and of the Puy de Tartaret, near Neckers. The rivers have even in some cases, as the Sioule, near Chalucet. cut through not only the basalt, which dispossessed them of their ancient channels, but have actually eaten fifty feet into the subjacent gneiss; yet the cone, an incoherent mass of scoriæ and spongy ejectamenta, stands unmolested. Had the waters once risen, even for a day, so high as to reach the level of the base of one of these cones,—had there been a single flood fifty or sixty feet in height, since the last eruption occurred, a great part of these volcanoes must inevitably have been swept away."

Here we are told that a stream, which had been turned out of its original course by an eruption of lava, has hollowed out for itself a new one, not only wearing away the hard basalt that had filled up the valley, but eating into the solid gneiss beneath. The formation of this new channel must have required a very lengthened period for its completion. According to Sir Charles's method of calculation, it must have taken some ten or twelve thousand years at least. At the same time, the piles of scoriæ and ashes that cover the crater remain undisturbed. Hence he concludes that "the waters have not once risen, even for a day, so high as to reach the level of the base of one of these cones," otherwise "a great part of them must inevitably have been swept away."

The language here employed leaves it somewhat doubtful whether the writer refers to the waters of a mountain torrent sweeping over the volcanic cones, or to the occurrence of a flood such as that which Moses describes as having covered the earth in the days of Noah. In his "Principles of Geology," chap. 45, his meaning is more distinctly expressed. He there says,—

"We may be enabled to infer, from the integrity of such conical hills of incoherent materials, that no flood can have passed over the countries where they are situated since their formation."

In another publication, which we have not had an opportunity of examining, his opinions, according to the account of Bishop Colenso, are still more decidedly expressed. The bishop says, in the introduction to his work on the Pentateuch :—

"My own knowledge of some branches of science—of geology in particular—had been much increased since I left England;

and as I now know for certain, on geological grounds, a fact of which I had only misgivings before, viz., that a *universal* deluge, such as the Bible manifestly speaks of, could not possibly have taken place in the way described in the Book of Genesis. I refer especially to the circumstance, well known to all geologists (see Lyell's ' Elementary Geology,' pp. 197, 198), that volcanic hills exist of immense extent in Auvergne and Languedoc, which must have been formed ages before the Noachian deluge, and which are covered with light and loose substances, pumice stone, &c., that must have been swept away by a flood, but do not exhibit the slightest sign of having ever been so disturbed. Of course, I am well aware that some have attempted to show that Noah's deluge was only a partial one; but such attempts have ever seemed to me to be made in the very teeth of the Scripture statements, which are as plain and explicit as words can possibly be."

In this extract we have, in the first place, the allegation that a deluge, such as Moses describes the Noachian deluge to have been, could not have taken place at the time which he assigns as the date of its occurrence. In the next place, we have the information that the Hebrew narrative being inconsistent with the discoveries of science, must be set aside. Bishop Colenso, accordingly, tells us that it was the incongruity which he found between the facts of geology and the statements of Scripture, that more especially influenced him in renouncing his belief in the inspiration of the author of the Pentateuch. Sir C. Lyell, led, we presume, by a similar process of reasoning, has come to a similar conclusion. He says, p. 380 :—

" True history and chronology are the creation, as it were, of yesterday. Thus the First Olympiad is generally regarded as the earliest date on which we can rely, in the past annals of mankind—only 772 years before the Christian era."

We deny the accuracy of the assertion, that a deluge, such as Moses describes the flood of Noah to have been, could not have taken place at the time which he assigns as the date of its occurrence, and maintain that the whole of Sir Charles's argument rests on a palpable mistake.

The effect produced by water on any substance exposed to its action depends on the rapidity with which the water is moving. We see the effect of the violent action of water when the river, swollen with the melting snow or heavy fall of rain, comes down as a sweeping flood, levels the dwellings of man by its impetuous force, tears up and carries away the trees of the forest, and covers the plain with banks of gravel and sand. We see it again when the sea, tossed by the tempest, dashes on the shore, and, by its repeated assaults, wears the rocks into rugged precipices, and hollows them out into caverns. Such are the effects of water when put into violent agitation.

We must not, however, attribute to water at rest, or only gently flowing, the same destructive influence that it exerts when violently agitated. The breakers, dashing against the shore, wear away the rock, and grind its fragments into gravel and sand ; but in the deep water, underneath the line to which the influence of the wave extends, no such destructive agency is found. There the most fragile shell remains uninjured, and the zoophyte expands its filmy arms and fears no evil. In the ocean, in curious contrast to the condition of political society, the upper portion is unceasingly restless, and its tendency is levelling and destructive, but the under portion is conservative and calm.

There is a very wide difference between the effect that is produced when anything is sunk in the still water of the deep, and that which results when it is exposed to the continuous action of the waves. The one is so small that it is hardly appreciable; the other is so great, as clearly to show the force of the billows to be one of the most formidable agencies in nature. Abundance of facts might be adduced to show that this is the case. A ship containing treasure sprung a leak, and sank in water so deep that the influence of the billows could not affect it. The depth, however, to which it sank, did not exceed the distance to which daring divers may descend. Sometime afterwards a diver went down to examine it, and found not only the vessel entire, but the glasses standing on the cabin table as the steward had left them. In such an instance as this we see the effect of a simple submergence under the deep. On the other hand, when a ship, even of the strongest construction, runs aground on a sand-bank, though it may not have sustained the slightest injury from the concussion, if a gale springs up before it can be got afloat again, it will be broken in pieces, and its strongest timbers will be scattered in wild confusion on the shore.

If the volcanic cones of Auvergne had been subjected to the continuous action of the billows,—in
other words, if they had formed for any length of time
a part of the ocean's shore, they would undoubtedly
have been swept away; but they may have been sunk
once and again beneath the deep without a single
cinder having been moved.

Islands that have been formed by the eruption of
submarine volcanoes afford a good illustration of our
present argument.   The cinders, stones, and ashes
cast up, have sometimes been known to form an
island several miles in extent, and two or three hundred feet in height.   In the course of a few months,
the upper portion, acted on by the billows, was swept
away, the island disappeared, and the ocean resumed
its domain.   The lower portion, however, was not
spread evenly over the bottom.   Underneath the line
which limits the action of the waves there was nothing
to disturb its repose.   It therefore retained its position, and forms a shoal.

The researches of geologists supply us with abundant
answers to the objections we are now considering.
For instance, we are informed that in many of the
ancient strata they find the footprints left by birds
and reptiles on the shore; while in others they can
trace the impressions made by the drops of falling rain.
Now, we ask, by what means was the preservation of
these perishable memorials of bygone ages effected?
They owe their preservation to their having been
covered over with water.   If they had been left ex-

posed to the sun and air, all trace of them would
speedily have vanished; but over the marks made on
the sand a mass of turbid water was gently spread,
and the mud it contained falling softly to the bottom,
formed a thin layer over the whole. This was followed
by a deposit of sand, and the whole was afterwards
converted into stone. It happens, however, that there
is no coherence between the sandstone and the film of
indurated mud. When the upper bed of sandstone,
therefore, is removed, the figures impressed on that
which is beneath can readily be traced. If in such
cases as these a covering over with water has been
the means of preserving these fragile impressions made
on the sand, it is not surely to be regarded as a thing
impossible* that mountain masses of volcanic scoriæ,
which have for untold ages resisted the effects of falling rain and atmospheric influence, should have been
buried beneath the deep, without being scattered in
disorder, or altogether swept away.

A gentle and gradual submergence of the earth
under the water, such as the Noachian deluge is represented to have been, if unaccompanied by any tempest
of the ocean, or violent convulsion of nature, would, in
fact, have no perceptible effect in moving even the
friable soil that covers the surface of the field. It
would scarcely disturb the mud lying at the bottom of
the pool; and if followed by a restoration of the land
to its former level without any intervening deposit, it
would leave no trace whatever of its having occurred.

V.

THE TIME REQUIRED FOR THE GROWTH OF PEAT.

ANOTHER of the arguments on which Sir Charles relies in proof of the antiquity of man rests on the thickness of some beds of peat, in which remains of human art have been found.

Passing by some allusions in the previous chapters, we find in chapter seventh a somewhat lengthened disquisition. After describing the upper and lower level gravels of the Somme, to which we have already referred, he gives an account of the peat :—

" Newer than these is the peat, which is from ten to thirty feet in thickness. . . . This substance occupies the lower part of the valley far above Amiens, and below Abbeville as far as the sea. It has already been stated to be in some places thirty feet thick, and is even occasionally more. . . . It belongs to the Recent Period, all the embedded mammalia, as well as shells, being of the same species as those now inhabiting Europe.

" The workmen who cut peat, or dredge it up from the bottom of swamps and ponds, declare that in the course of their lives none of the hollows which they have found, or caused by ex-tracting peat, have ever been refilled, even to a small extent. They deny, therefore, that peat grows. This, as M. Boucher de Perthes observes, is a mistake ; but it implies that the increase in one generation is not very appreciable by the unscientific."

M. B. de Perthes, according to this extract, seems

to entertain the idea that peat grows at the bottom of pools, and that wherever it is formed it is the effect of some very slow and mysterious process. A few observations on its nature and growth will enable us to test the accuracy of his calculations.

Peat, in its chemical composition as well as in its appearance, resembles the charcoal which is produced when vegetable substances are exposed to heat. Like charcoal, it is not only itself very little affected by ordinary atmospheric influences, but possesses an antiseptic quality which tends to prevent the decay of other bodies that may be surrounded by it. These properties are familiarly known. A piece of peat, unmixed with vegetable fibres, when laid on the surface of the ground, and exposed to the summer's drought and to the winter's rain, will remain for many years unchanged. Vegetable substances, the wood, for instance, of the oak, the fir, and the alder, the nut of the hazel, and the acorn, when embedded in peat, retain their form and consistency for a very lengthened period. Even the bodies of animals, in similar circumstances, will resist for a considerable time the progress of decomposition. In these particulars the properties of peat present a striking contrast to those of the *humus* or vegetable mould, which is produced by the decay of other classes of vegetable substances. That mould, exposed freely to atmospheric influence, speedily wastes away, and accelerates rather than retards the decomposition of other bodies.

The manner in which peat is produced has not, perhaps, received that attention which is necessary for a full explanation of the subject, but some particulars are abundantly clear. That the mosses and lichens, and other plants which are allied to them, when exposed to decay, especially in moist situations, are transformed into peat, has long been familiarly known. It has not, we believe, been so generally remarked, that the roots and other underground parts of almost all the plants indigenous to boggy soil undergo a similar change. If we examine those roots, which from their size allow us more easily to trace the process of transformation, we frequently find that even when the central part appears to be fresh, the bark or outer skin has been converted into peat. Some roots of a larger size and spongy texture have their bark transformed into a substance that resembles coal, while the interior is filled with a soft pulpy mass. When they are pressed together by the weight of matter that accumulates above them, these larger roots, thus changed, may be not inaptly compared to ribbons of black silk. We may in passing remark, that geologists are aware that the stigmaria and other marsh-loving plants of former eras underwent a similar transformation.

This process goes on with the greatest certainty, and with the greatest rapidity, in those moist situations for which the plants are naturally adapted; but wherever they can vegetate, whether the ground be moist or dry, they manifest the same peat producing tendency. If we pull up the stem of the horse-tail, *equisetum,* in the thoroughly drained and cultivated field, or the rhizoma of the marsh fern from the fernery, we find the underground bark covered with a film of incipient peat. On one occasion we observed that a plant of the globe flower, *trollius europeus*, which for several years had occupied a place in the flower border, and had in that time formed a matted turf several inches in thickness, had been affected by a blight, by which the greater part of the plant had been killed. On lifting the part decayed we found it almost wholly changed into peat, and then recollected that the globe flower very frequently constitutes no inconsiderable portion of the flora of our bogs.

As is the case with every member of the vegetable family, the plants we speak of will grow most vigorously when the situation is favourable to their peculiar nature. Without an adequate supply of moisture their growth is dwarfed and stunted. Without shelter it is but slow. If in addition to moisture and shelter there be an abundant supply of appropriate nutriment, their vegetation will be luxuriant.

The increase of peat depends, of course, on the growth of the plants that produce it. If the plants be destroyed, as they seem to have been in the cases to which M. Boucher de Perthes referred, no peat can be formed. The workmen were perfectly correct when they said that it did not grow at the bottom of pools, and its increase, in the circumstances they spoke of, could not have been appreciated even by the most "scientific." In a marsh surrounded by the forest, and covered in autumn with the drifting leaves, or in a water-fed meadow, such as the valley of the Somme seems to have been in former times, over which the debris of the surrounding woods are spread by the winter floods, the growth of the marsh-loving plants will be vigorous, and the accumulation of peat will be large.

Another circumstance would heighten this effect in situations like the valley of the Somme. The particles of peat are very minute, and easily diffused through water. Every shower that falls on a mossy district carries off a portion, and the inky colour of the streams that flow through it shows the large amount that they contain. When these streams are spread over a level plain, and the water is filtered in passing through the matted vegetation that covers the ground, a large proportion of the peaty matter they bring down is left behind, and will add very considerably to the thickness of the deposit.

Sir Charles gives us the following estimate of the time required for the growth of peat :—

" The antiquary finds near the surface Gallo-Roman remains, and still deeper, Celtic weapons of the stone period. But the depth at which Roman works of art occur varies in different places, and is no sure test of age, because in some parts of the swamps, especially near the river, the peat is often so fluid that heavy substances may sink through it, carried down by their own gravity. In one case, however, M. Boucher de Perthes observed several large flat dishes of Roman pottery lying in a horizontal position in the peat, the shape of which must have prevented them from sinking or penetrating through the underlying peat. Allowing about fourteen centuries for the growth of the superincumbent vegetable matter, he calculated that the thickness gained in a hundred years would be no more than three French centimetres. This rate of increase would demand so many tens of thousands of years for the formation of the entire thickness of thirty feet, that we must hesitate before adopting it as a chronometric scale. Yet, by multiplying observations of this kind, and bringing one to bear upon and check another, we may eventually succeed in obtaining data for estimating the age of the peaty deposit." (P. 111.)

We are not told what the circumstances were on which M. de Perthes founded his calculation that the peaty deposit increases at the rate of three centimetres, or an inch and fifth, in a century. We have nothing by which we can test the probability of his speculation, which Sir Charles seems so highly to esteem, and to which he again refers in page 144, in page 205, and again in page 373. We are happy, however, that we have an author on whose accuracy we can place much greater confidence, to whom we can refer :—

" In the moss of Hatfield, as well as in that of Kincardine, in Scotland, and several others, Roman roads have been found covered to the depth of eight feet by peat. All the coins, axes, arms, and other utensils found in British and French mosses, are also Roman : so that a considerable portion of the European peat bogs are evidently not more ancient than the days of Julius Cæsar. Nor can any vestiges of the ancient forests, described by that general, along the line of the great Roman way in Britain, be discovered except in the ruined trunks of trees in the peat."

The Roman road in Scotland here spoken of as covered with a depth of eight feet of peat, was laid bare, if we recollect aright, some fifty or sixty years

D

ago. If we suppose it to have been made in the year A.D. 200, at which date the Romans pushed their conquests farthest into Britain, the rate of growth in the peat, assuming it to have been uniform from the time of the Romans, would be six inches in a century, not an inch and fifth, as M. de Perthes calculates.

In the same chapter we have recorded an instance of much more rapid increase :—

" We also learn that the overthrow of a forest by a storm, about the middle of the seventeenth century, gave rise to a peat moss in Lochbroom, in Ross-shire, where, in less than half a century after the fall of the trees, the inhabitants dug peat."

Peat is not so scarce in Ross-shire as to induce the people to dig it unless it were at least eighteen inches thick. This would, therefore, give a rate of increase of three feet in a century.

The quotations we have given are from Sir Charles Lyell's former work on the " Principles of Geology." We presume that every unbiassed reader will agree with us in preferring the facts recorded by so accurate an observer as the author of the " Principles of Geology," to the vague speculations of M. Boucher de Perthes.

We further remark, that we are not required to account for the formation of peat of the average thickness of thirty feet. That thickness is the maximum, found only in the deeper hollows, into which, we may presume, sediment had been carried by the river floods.

VI.

RELICS OF MAN IN DEPOSITS OF MUD.

IN various parts of the world we find rivers bringing down great quantities of sand and mud, which gradually fill up the valleys through which the rivers flow, and form deltas at their mouths. Intermingled with these deposits, bones belonging to the human frame and works of art are occasionally found. The depth at which some of these relics have been discovered, has induced some speculative geologists to maintain that man must have been an inhabitant of the earth for a much longer period than that which the Mosaic chronology assigns to the human era.

Sir Charles describes several of these alleged evidences of man's antiquity, to two of which we shall refer :—

" In the latitude of Vicksburgh, the broad alluvial plain of the Mississippi is bounded on its eastern side by a table-land about two hundred feet higher than the river, and extending twelve miles eastward, with a gentle upward slope. This elevated platform ends abruptly in a line of perpendicular cliffs or bluffs, the base of which is continually undermined by the great river. The table-land consists of yellow loam overlying the tertiary strata.

" Owing to the destructible nature of this loam, every stream-

let flowing over the platform has cut for itself, in its way to the
Mississippi, a deep gully or ravine; and this erosion has of late
years proceeded with accelerated speed, ascribable, in some degree, to the partial clearing of the native forest, but partly also
to the effects of the earthquake of 1811–12. By that convulsion
the region around Natchez was rudely shaken and much fissured.
One of the narrow valleys due to this fissuring is now called the
Mammoth Ravine. Though no less than seven miles long, and
in some parts sixty feet deep, I was assured by a resident pro-
prietor that it had no existence before 1812.

" From a clayey deposit immediately below the yellow loam,
bones of the mastodon, megalonyx, equus, bos, and others, some
of extinct, and others presumed to be of living species, had been
detached, and had fallen to the base of the cliffs. Mingled with
the rest, the pelvic bone of a man, *os innominatum*, was obtained
by Dr Dickson of Natchez, in whose collection I saw it It appeared to be quite in the same state of preservation, and was of
the same black colour as the other fossils, and was believed to
have come like them from a depth of about thirty feet from the
surface. I suggested, as a possible explanation of this association of a human bone with remains of the mastodon and megalonyx, that the former may possibly have been derived from the
vegetable soil at the top of the cliff, whereas the remains of the
extinct mammalias were dislodged from a lower position, and
both may have fallen into the same heap at the bottom of the
ravine. The pelvic bone might have acquired its black colour
by having lain in a dark superficial peaty soil, common in that
region. . . . . . No doubt, had the bone belonged to any recent
mammifer other than man, such a theory would never have been
resorted to; but so long as we have only one isolated case, and
are without the testimony of a geologist who was present to behold the bone, when still engaged in the matrix, and to extract
it with his own hands, it is allowable to suspend our judgment
as to the high antiquity of the fossil.

" If I was right in calculating that the present delta of the
Mississippi has required, as a minimum of time, more than one

hundred thousand years for its growth, it would follow, if the claims of the Natchez man to have coexisted with the mastodon are admitted, that North America was peopled more than a thousand centuries ago by the human race." (P. 204.)

We do not require to make any remark on these quotations. We give them as an example of the loose, inconclusive evidence with which a great part of Sir Charles's work is filled.

Another instance of human relics in alluvial deposits deserves more particular notice, in consequence of the discussion to which some years ago it gave rise :—

" Some new facts of high interest, illustrating the geology of the alluvial land of Egypt, was brought to light between the years 1851 and 1854, in consequence of the investigations suggested to the Royal Society, by Mr Leonard Horner, and which was partly carried out at the expense of the Society, and afterwards continued by the princely liberality of the Viceroy.

" The results of chief importance, arising out of this inquiry, were obtained from two sets of shafts and borings, sunk at intervals in lines crossing the great valley from east to west. One of them consisted of no less than fifty-one pits and artesian preparations, made where the valley is sixteen miles from side to side, about eight miles above the apex of the delta. The other line of borings and pits, twenty-seven in number, was in the parallel of Memphis, where the valley is only five miles broad.

" All the remains of organic bodies, such as land shells and the bones of quadrupeds, found during the excavations, belonged to living species. No vestiges of extinct mammalia were anywhere detected.

" In some instances the excavations were on a large scale for the first sixteen or twenty-four feet, in which cases jars, vases, pots, or small human figures in burnt clay, a copper knife, and other entire articles, were dug up; but when water, soaking through from the Nile, was reached, the boring instrument used was too small to allow of more than fragments of works of art to be brought up. Pieces of burnt brick and pottery were extracted almost everywhere, and from all depths, even when they sank sixty feet below the surface in the central parts of the valley.

" M. Gerard, of the French expedition to Egypt, supposed the average rate of the increase of Nile mud on the plain, between Assouan and Cairo, to be five English inches in a century. This assumption, according to Mr Horner, is very vague, and founded on insufficient data,—the amount of matter thrown down by the waters in different parts of the plain varying so much, that to strike an average with any approach to accuracy must be most difficult. Were we to assume six inches to a century, the burnt brick met with at a depth of sixty feet would be 12,000 years old.

" Another fragment of red brick was found by Linant Bey in a boring seventy-two feet deep, two hundred metres from the river. M. Rosiere, in the great French work on Egypt, has estimated the mean rate of deposit of sediment in the delta at two inches and three lines in a century. Were we to take two and a-half inches, a work of art seventy-two feet deep must have been buried 30,000 years ago." (P. 38.)

In remarking on this statement we observe, in the first place, that while we have set before us the estimates of MM. Gerard and Rosiere, we have no information given us of the data on which they proceeded. Until we know the facts on which they rested, their conclusions are not admissible as proof.

In the next place, even if we allow that their calculations are correct in reference to the amount of modern deposit, we are not entitled to conclude that the present rate has never been exceeded. Many circumstances, of which we are ignorant, may have diminished the amount of sediment carried along by the stream. There is, in fact, good reason for supposing that the quantity formerly deposited was larger than it is at present. In the days of Egypt's prosperity, the skill of its engineers, and the labours of its dense population, were earnestly and assiduously employed in devising and executing expedients for retaining the muddy water brought down by the annual flood, in order to fertilise the soil. In these circumstances, the deposit retained must have been very much greater than it is at present, when the inhabitants are comparatively few, and the cultivation of the land in a great measure neglected.

We would more especially remark, that all these speculations proceed on the supposition that there has been no subterranean agency at work affecting the general level of the country. It needs no lengthened argument to show, that if the country has been subjected to elevations and depressions, through the operation of internal forces, any calculation which rests on the hypothesis of a uniform rate of deposit must be fallacious. If the upper part of the valley were to sink, while the lower remained stationary, the Nile would very speedily fill up the hollow thus formed with the mud which is now carried down to the sea. If, on the other hand, the upper part of the valley were to rise, or to remain at its former level, while the lower part was depressed, the water in flowing over it would probably carry off more than it brought down,

and reduce instead of augmenting the thickness of the
soil.

Sir Gardner Wilkinson tells us that he has been led
to infer that there has been a sinking of some parts of
the land of Egypt, from the position in the delta, on
the shores near Alexandria, of the tombs called
Cleopatra's Baths, which cannot have been originally
built so as to be exposed to the sea which now fills
them, but must have stood on land above the level of
the Mediterranean. He adduces, as additional signs
of subsidence, some ruined towns now half under water
in the Lake of Menzaleh, and channels of ancient arms
of the Nile submerged with their banks beneath the
waters of that lagoon.

If we admit the accuracy of these observations,
which does not seem to admit of a doubt, we must
look on Egypt as a country that has been subjected,
like many others, to subsidence and elevation, through
the action of subterranean forces.

The depression of the parts of the delta that adjoin
the sea, to which he here refers, may very probably
have been the means of reducing the deposit left in
the upper part of the valley. In the earlier ages an
opposite process would appear to have gone on. Herodotus tells us that the Egyptians enclosed with embankments the areas on which they had built their
temples and monuments, and that, even in his day,
these spots appeared sunk, and could be looked down
into from the surrounding grounds. This account of
the Greek historian suggests the idea of such a depres-

sion of the sites on which the temples stood, as made it necessary to enclose these sacred edifices with embankments to protect them from the annual floods.

Whatever value we may attach to these suppositions, Sir G. Wilkinson's observations make it plain that Egypt is subject to changes of level through the agency of internal forces; and it is therefore evident, that the estimated rate of annual deposit, the " chronometric scale " of the Egyptologists, of which some years ago we heard so much, possesses no value whatever.

VII.

SUCCESSIVE GENERATIONS OF TREES.

THE time required for the growth of forests is another circumstance on which Sir Charles rests some of his arguments in support of his hypothesis :—

" The deposits of peat in Denmark, varying in depth from ten to thirty feet, have been formed in hollows in the northern drift. The lowest stratum, two or three feet thick, consists of swamp peat, composed chiefly of moss or sphagnum, above which lies another growth of peat, not made up exclusively of aquatic or swamp plants. Around the borders of the bogs, and at various depths in them, lie trunks of trees, especially of the Scotch fir, often three feet in diameter, which must have grown on the margin of the mosses and fallen into them. This tree is not now, nor has ever been in historical times a native of Denmark, and when introduced there has not thriven. It appears that the Scotch fir was afterwards supplanted by the sessile variety of the common oak, of which many trunks occur in the peat at higher levels than the pines ; and still higher, the pedunculated variety of the same oak occurs, with the alder, birch, and hazel. The oak has now in its turn been almost superseded by the common beech.

" By collecting and studying a vast variety of articles of human workmanship preserved in peat, the Danish antiquaries have succeeded in establishing a chronological succession of periods, which they have called the ages of stone, of bronze, and of iron, named from the materials which have each in their turn served for the fabrication of implements.

" The age of stone coincided with the period of the first vegetation, or that of the Scotch fir, and in part at least with the
second vegetation, or that of the oak. But a considerable portion of the oak period coincided with the age of bronze, for
swords and shields of that metal have been taken out of peat in
which oaks abound. The age of iron corresponded more nearly
with that of the beech." (P. 10.)

" What may be the antiquity of the earliest human remains
preserved in the Danish peat, cannot be estimated in centuries
with any approach to accuracy. In the first place, in going back
to the bronze age, we already find ourselves beyond the reach
of history, or even of tradition. In the time of the Romans,
the Danish isles were covered as now with magnificent beech
forests. Nowhere in the world does this tree flourish more
luxuriantly than in Denmark, and eighteen centuries seem to
have done little or nothing towards modifying the character of
the forest vegetation. Yet in the antecedent bronze period
there were no beech trees, or at most but a few stragglers, the
country being then covered with oak. In the age of stone the
Scotch fir prevailed, and already there were human inhabitants
in those old pine forests. How many generations of each species
of tree flourished in succession before the pine was supplanted
by the oak, and the oak by the beech, can be but vaguely con-
jectured." (P. 16.)

In this extract Sir Charles does not directly affirm,
that since " eighteen centuries seem to have done little
or nothing towards modifying the character of the
forest vegetation," we must allow some great, indefinite time before we can account for the varieties of
trees found in the Danish peat ; but this is the conclusion to which his argument naturally leads. On
the other hand, we think that we arrive at a more
legitimate inference from the facts laid before us,

when we affirm, that if eighteen centuries have produced no change on the forest vegetation of Denmark,
the changes formerly experienced cannot have been
produced by the lapse of time, but by some cause
affecting the climate or soil. And when we observe
in our own country the beech growing in the sheltered
plain, the oak clothing the sides of the mountains,
and the pine trees covering their brow, we look on
the varied products dug out of the Danish peat as
evidencing merely successive stages in the amelioration of the climate. That amelioration, as we formerly
endeavoured to show, is not to be accounted for by
ascribing some strange mysterious power to a long
succession of ages, but by supposing a change in the
direction of the great Gulf Stream, a depression of
the general level of the country, or some other effect
such as might be produced by the operation of subterranean forces. As we have no reason for concluding that these forces were regulated in prehistoric times
by the *two and half feet rule* which Sir Charles assigns
to them, we see no necessity for supposing that any
very lengthened period was required for the successive
generations of pine tree, oak, and beech.

In another part of his volume Sir Charles directs
attention to America :—

"There are hundreds of large mounds in the basin of the
Mississippi, and especially in the valleys of the Ohio and its
tributaries, which have served some of them for temples, others
for outlook or defence, and others for sepulture. The unknown
people by whom they were constructed, judging by the form of

several skulls dug out of the burial-places, were of the Mexican or Toltecan race. Some of the earthworks embrace areas of fifty or a hundred acres, within a simple enclosure, and the solid contents of one mound are estimated at twenty millions of cubic feet. From several of these repositories pottery and ornamental sculpture have been taken, and various articles in silver and copper, also stone weapons, some composed of horn-stone unpolished, and much resembling the ancient flint implements found near Amiens.

" When I visited Marietta in 1842, Dr Hildreth took me to one of the mounds, and showed me where he had seen a tree growing in it, the trunk of which, when cut down, displayed eight hundred rings of annual growth. But the late General Harrison, President of the United States in 1841, who was well skilled in wood-craft, has remarked, in a memoir on this subject, that several generations of trees must have lived and died before the mounds could have been overspread with that variety of species which they supported when the white man first beheld them; for the number and kinds of trees were precisely the same as those which distinguished the neighbouring forest. ' We may be sure,' observed Harrison, ' that no trees were allowed to grow so long as the earthworks were in use; and when they were forsaken, the ground, like all newly cleared land in Ohio, would, for a time, be monopolised by one or two species of tree, such as the yellow locust and the black or white walnut. When the individuals which were the first to get possession of the ground had died out, one after the other, they would, in many cases, instead of being replaced by the same species, be succeeded (by virtue of the law which makes a rotation of crops profitable in agriculture) by other kinds, till at last, after a great number of centuries, several thousand years perhaps, the remarkable diversity of species, characteristic of North America, and far exceeding what is seen in European forests, would be established.' " (P. 61.)

We have here a variety of assumptions, but an utter

want of proof. " We may be sure," says Mr Harrison,
" that no trees were allowed to grow so long as the
earthworks were in use." We are sure of no such
thing: they may have been planted there for ornament or for shelter. We are told of the laws that
regulate the succession of trees in America,—and certainly they are very different from those that prevail
in Europe,—and of the thousands of years that must
elapse before certain changes can take place, but
where is the proof in support of the assertion?

Even if we grant all these suppositions, it must be
remarked that Mr Harrison's whole argument rests on
the assumption that the Ohian Toltecs, when they
removed from their old abodes, left their habitations
and enclosures in the same state as that of a modern
American clearing, when forsaken by its roving cultivator. There is no evidence whatever that this was
the case. There is no probability in the supposition.
They left a comparatively small piece of ground, in
the middle of the forest, some of it, perhaps, cultivated
as gardens—some of it as pasture—some of it, it may
be, planted with trees for shelter and shade—some
thrown up in mounds—and some covered with rubbish.
Preparation was thus made for receiving the seeds of
the trees growing around, whatever the situation might
be that their various natures required. These seeds
took root and grew. If eight hundred annual rings
have been reckoned in some of the trees thus produced,
we conclude that eight centuries, at least, have elapsed
since the emigration took place. This is all that the

facts related to us can fairly be regarded as proving. Anything further is merely unsupported conjecture.

In page 43 we have another American evidence of the antiquity of man :—

" Near New Orleans a large excavation has been made for gas-works, where a succession of beds, almost wholly made up of vegetable matter, has been passed through, such as we now see forming the cypress swamps in the neighbourhood. In this excavation, at the depth of sixteen feet from the surface, beneath four buried forests, superimposed one upon the other, the work-men are stated by Dr B. Dowler to have found some charcoal and a human skeleton, the cranium of which is said to belong to the aboriginal type of the Red Indian race. As the discovery in question had not been made when I saw the excavation in 1846, I cannot form an opinion as to the value of the chronolo-gical calculations which have led Dr Dowler to ascribe to the skeleton an antiquity of 50,000 years."

Here we are told of four successive generations of trees found in a cutting sixteen feet deep. The trees cannot have been very large, otherwise the mould in which they were embedded must have been deeper. If we were to assign to each generation two hundred years, and allow half that time for the mud brought down by the river to silt them up and form a new soil, and were thus to come to the conclusion, that the Indian, whose skeleton was there discovered, perished in the cypress swamp some ten or twelve hundred years ago, we would surely form a more probable con-jecture than the American savant, who ascribes to the skeleton an antiquity of fifty thousand years. It certainly does not seem a very difficult matter to form an opinion of chronological calculations that lead to conclusions so manifestly absurd.

VIII.

IMPROVEMENT IN THE USEFUL ARTS AMONG THE EARLY INHABITANTS OF EUROPE.

THERE is no part of Sir C. Lyell's work more interesting than the notices which we find interspersed
through its pages, illustrating the gradual advancement of the early Europeans in the useful arts. We
shall give the more important of these notices in what
may be regarded as an approach to chronological order.

Burial Place at Aurignac.—The town of Aurignac
is situated in the department of the Haute Garonne,
at the northern base of the Pyrenees. In the neighbourhood of this town, in 1852, a grotto was discovered,
which seems, in a remote age, to have served as a
burial-place. It appears to have been a natural cavern,
on the side of the hill, closed artificially by a heavy
slab of rock placed vertically against the entrance. In
the interior were the remains of seventeen skeletons,
young and old, belonging to a race of small stature.
Outside the cave there was a bed of charcoal and
ashes, seven inches thick, the remains, it has been
supposed, of funeral feasts held there in memory of
the departed. Among the ashes were a great variety
of bones and implements; amongst the latter, not

fewer than a hundred flint articles, knives, projectiles, sling stones, and chips. There was also found one of those silicious cores, or nuclei, with numerous facets, from which flint flakes had been struck off, seeming to prove that some instruments were occasionally manufactured on the spot. Among the bone implements, were arrows without barbs, and other tools, made of reindeer horn, and a bodkin formed out of the more compact horn of the roedeer. Scattered through the same ashes were the bones of the following animals, —cave bear, brown bear, badger, polecat, wild cat, cave hyæna, wolf, fox, mammoth, rhinoceros, horse, ass, stag, Irish deer, roebuck, reindeer, and bison. Inside of the cave, underneath the human remains, similar bones were found, besides some that appear to have belonged to the cave lion and pig. The bones of the herbivora were the most numerous; and all those on the outside of the grotto which had contained marrow, were invariably split open, as if for its extraction, many of them being also burnt.

Cavern in Devonshire.—At Brixham, near Torquay, a cavern has been discovered, through which water seems formerly to have flowed. In it implements of flint were found mingled with the remains of extinct animals; among them the mammoth, rhinoceros, cave bear, cave lion, cave hyæna, reindeer, and others not yet determined.

Cavern of Arcy-sur-Yonne.—In this cavern a series of deposits has lately been investigated by the Marquis de Vibraye, who discovered human bones in the

E

lowest of them, mixed with remains of quadrupeds of extinct and recent species. The lowest formation resembles the grey diluvium of Paris ; in it have been found the two branches of a human lower jaw, with teeth well preserved, and the bones of the mammoth, rhinoceros, cave bear, cave hyæna, and reindeer. Above the grey gravel is a bed of red alluvium, in which were embedded several flint knives, with bones of the reindeer and horse, but no extinct mammalia. Over this, in a higher bed of alluvium, were several polished hatchets of the more modern type, called '' celts ;'' and above all, loam, in which were Gallo-Roman antiquities.

Danish Shell Heaps.—'' At certain points along the shores of nearly all the Danish islands mounds may be seen, consisting chiefly of the cast away shells of the oyster, cockle, and other molluscs, now eaten by man. Scattered all through them are flint knives, hatchets, and other instruments of stone, horn, wood, and bone, with fragments of coarse pottery, mixed with charcoal and cinders, but never any implements of bronze or iron. The stone hatchets and knives had been sharpened by rubbing, and in this respect are one degree less rude than those found in France associated with the bones of extinct mammalia. There are no remains of any extinct species except of the wild bull, which are in such numbers as to prove that its flesh was a favourite food. As this animal was seen by Julius Cæsar, and survived long after his time, its presence does not prove the mounds to be of high antiquity. There are also bones of some carnivora, such as the lynx, fox, and wolf, but no signs of any domesticated animals except the dog. . . . . . The domestic ox, horse, and sheep, are wanting in the mounds, and are confined to that part of the Danish peat which grew in the ages of bronze and iron. . . . . . The relics of several deep sea species of fish, such as the herring, cod, and flounder, show that the ancient people must have ventured out to sea to catch fish far from land. . . . . . No trace of grain has been discovered, nor any other indication of an acquaintance with agriculture. . . . . . Skulls have been obtained from tumuli of the stone period, believed to be contemporaneous with the mounds. These skulls are small and round, and have a prominent ridge over the orbits of the eyes, showing that the ancient race was of small stature, with round heads and overhanging eyebrows—in short, they bore a considerable resemblance to the modern Laplanders. The skulls of the bronze age found in the Danish peat, and those of the iron period, are of an elongated form and larger size." (P. 16.)

Swiss Lake Dwellings.—" In the shallow parts of many Swiss lakes, where there is a depth of no more than from five to fifteen feet of water, ancient wooden piles are observed at the bottom, sometimes worn down to the surface of the mud, sometimes projecting slightly above it. These have evidently supported villages, nearly all of them of unknown date; but the most ancient certainly belonged to the age of stone, for hundreds of implements resembling those of the Danish shell mounds and peat mosses have been dredged up from the mud into which the piles were driven.

" The earliest historical account of such habitations is that given by Herodotus of a Thracian tribe, who dwelt in the year 520 B.C. in Prasias, a small mountain lake of Pæonia. Their habitations were constructed on platforms raised above the lake and resting on piles. They were connected with the shore by a narrow causeway of similar formation. Such platforms must have been of considerable extent, for the Pæonians lived there with their families and horses. . . . . .

" The number of sites which have already been enumerated in Switzerland is truly wonderful. They occur on the large lakes of Constance, Zurich, Geneva, and Neufchatel, and on most of the smaller ones. Some are exclusively of the stone age, others of the bronze period.

" One of the sites first studied by the Swiss antiquaries was the small lake of Moosedorf, near Berne, where implements of stone, horn, and bone, but none of metal, were obtained. Although the flint here employed must have come from a distance, probably from the south of France, the chippings of the material are in such profusion as to imply that there was a manufactory of implements on the spot. Here also, as in several other settlements, hatchets and wedges of jade have been observed, of a kind said not to occur in Switzerland, or the adjoining parts of Europe, and which some mineralogists would fain derive from the East; amber, also, which it is supposed was imported from the shores of the Baltic.

" At Wangen, near Stein, on Lake Constance, is another of the lake dwellings, where hatchets of serpentine and greenstone, and arrow heads of quartz, have been met with. Here, also, remains of a kind of cloth, supposed to be of flax, not woven, but plaited, have been detected. Professor Heer has recognised lumps of carbonised wheat and barley, and flat-round cakes of bread, clearly showing that in the stone period the lake dwellers cultivated all these cereals, besides having domesticated the dog, the ox, the sheep, and the goat.

" Near Morges, on the Lake of Geneva, a settlement of the bronze period, no less than forty hatchets of that metal have been dredged up. . . . . . In some few of the aquatic stations, a mixture of bronze and iron implements and works of art have been observed, including coins and medals of bronze and silver, struck at Marseilles, and of Greek manufacture.

" It is remarkable that as yet all the settlements of the bronze period are confined to Western and Central Switzerland. In the more Eastern lakes those of the stone period alone have as yet been discovered." (P. 21.)

The wild mammalia whose bones have been found in connection with these lake dwellings are all of existing species. The domesticated species comprise the dog, horse, ass, pig, goat, sheep, and several varieties of the ox.

In the settlements belonging to the earliest age of stone the habits of the hunter predominated over those of the shepherd, and the flesh of animals slain in the chase was more eaten than the flesh of the domestic cattle and sheep. This was afterwards reversed in the later stone period, and in the age of bronze.

" Amidst all this profusion of animal remains extremely few bones of man have been discovered; and only one skull, dredged up from Meilen, on the Lake of Zurich, of the early stone period, seems as yet to have been carefully examined. This specimen exhibits, instead of the small and rounded form proper to the Danish peat mosses, a type much more like that now prevailing in Switzerland, which is intermediate between the long headed and short headed form." (P. 26.)

These extracts give us a very interesting picture of the life and manners of the early inhabitants of Europe. There were, in the first place, a race of hunters, armed with weapons of stone, and living in a great measure on the flesh of animals now extinct. There were, in the next place, the inhabitants of the Swiss lake dwellings, armed at first like the others with implements of stone, and feeding almost exclusively on animals slain in the chase, at a later period employing instruments of bronze, and feeding on the flesh of animals which they had domesticated. The aborigines of Denmark are represented as belonging to a race differing both in form and in pursuits. It is not at all improbable that in the earlier periods of their history they were contemporary with the hunter tribes of Britain and Gaul. The absence of the bones of the larger mammalia in their refuse heaps, may

only indicate that these animals, though inhabiting
the Continent, were not found in the Danish islands;
or, that the people, like the Esquimaux, their representatives in the present day, sought their livelihood
on the sea, while the others, like the red races of
America, sought theirs in the forest and the field.

In these statements we have abundant evidence to
show us that the early inhabitants of Europe, in prehistoric times, had made very decided progress, both
in their manufactures and in their manner of life.
The substitution of bronze for flint, and of iron for
bronze, in the fabrication of their weapons, was one
very manifest indication of improvement. The introduction of domesticated animals, and the practice of
agriculture, was another. We are not sure, however,
that we can agree with the antiquarians who look on
the polishing of their stone weapons as a sign of
advancement. So long as the mammoth and other
larger game formed the objects of their chase, we may
suppose that the hunters would attack them as the
Africans of the present day attack the elephant. According to the account given by Dr Livingston, the
negroes on such occasions gather together in large
bodies, armed with bundles of spears, which they dart
at their prey in such numbers, that, though no one
inflicts a mortal injury, the unwieldy brute falls a
victim to the multitude of his wounds. For such a
purpose as this, the flakes of flint, as struck from its
original core, and brought into shape by the strokes of
the hammer, with its edges sharp and jagged, would

form as effective a weapon as the material could supply. We are rather inclined to regard the polished
stone as having been, in all periods, the hatchet held
in the hand, while the rough and jagged flint pointed
the spear thrown at the prey. After the larger mammalia became extinct, and the inhabitants had to depend for subsistence on animals whose defence lay in
the speed of their flight, rather than in their strength,
the spears would be discontinued, and arrows pointed
with bone or horn would be preferred.

However this may be, we do not think it necessary
to infer that it required many ages to produce these
ameliorations in their arts and their condition. The
improvements we refer to may have originated in two
different causes: The original population may have
advanced in the arts of life ; or a more civilised race
may have conquered them, and taken possession of
their territory.

If we adopt the first of these suppositions, we are
prepared to maintain that the introduction of more
efficient weapons, of domesticated animals, and of the
simpler forms of agricultural labour, does not require
any very lengthened period of time. The South Sea
Islanders, who had been for ages accustomed to weapons of flint and bone, laid them aside so soon as
Europeans brought them a supply of iron. Many of
them, taught by missionaries, or following the example
of European settlers, are now possessed of flocks, and
herds, and cultivated fields. The early inhabitants of
Europe, judging from their cerebral development,

were by no means destitute of intellectual capacity. We may therefore suppose that, like the South Sea Islanders, they would lay aside their weapons of stone whenever traders from the south brought them for sale implements of bronze, or supplied them with the metal of which to make them. In like manner, if colonists, such as the Greeks and Carthaginians are represented as having sent out, were settled among them, they would imitate the customs and learn the arts of their more cultivated visitors. It is not " many centuries " since the Tahitians first saw the face of a white man, and yet we find their civilization in a higher state of advancement than that of the ancient Swiss.

We think, however, that the second supposition is the more probable, and that the aboriginal hunter tribes had their country invaded by more civilised races, whose superiority in arms and discipline would give them a speedy victory. When we find the rude implements of a savage people in a bed of gravel or mud, and more elaborately formed articles lying above them, this shows that the one had been deposited before the other, but it affords no data for determining how long the period was that intervened between them. Some future geologist may find in the bed of an Australian river the flint implements of the aborigines, with the fragments of British manufactures lying above them. The position in which the remains are found would justify him in concluding that a people, far advanced in civilization, had taken possession of a country formerly occupied by an uncultivated race; but it would not entitle him to say, that this change in the population required the lapse of many ages in order to explain its occurrence.

We therefore consider the estimate made by Sir Charles, of the time required for introducing improvements in the useful arts among the early inhabitants of Europe, as resting on assumptions which the facts he adduces are not sufficient to warrant.

IX.

THE PRIMEVAL CONDITION OF MAN.

THE statement made by the President of the British
Association, when he said that, "it seems no longer
possible to doubt that the human race has existed on
the earth, in a barbarian state, for a period far exceeding the limit of the historical record," assumes two
things as placed beyond the possibility of doubt : that
man existed on the earth for a period far exceeding
the limit of the historical record, and that this existence was at the first in a barbarian state.

We have already considered the arguments brought
forward to prove the great antiquity of man ; we now
proceed to examine the other part of the President's
assertion. We quote, as before, the words of Sir
Charles Lyell :—

" Some modern ethnologists, in accordance with the philosophers of antiquity, have assumed that men first fed on the fruits
of the earth, before even a stone implement, or the simplest form
of canoe, had been invented. They may, it is said, have begun
their career in some fertile island in the tropics, where the
warmth of the air was such that no clothing was needed, and
where there were no wild beasts to endanger their safety. But
as soon as their numbers increased, they would be forced to migrate into regions less secure, and blest with a less genial
climate. Contests would soon arise for the possession of the

most fertile lands, where game or pasture abounded, and their energies and inventive powers would be called forth, so that, at length, they would make progress in the arts." (P. 386.)

" The opinion entertained generally by the classical writers of Greece and Rome, that man, in the first stage of his existence, was but just removed from the brutes, is faithfully expressed by Horace in his celebrated lines :—   ·

"'Quum prorepserunt primis animalia terris,' &c. (Snt. lib. i. 3, 99.)

" The picture of transmutation given in these verses, however severe and contemptuous the strictures lavishly bestowed on it by Christian commentators, accords singularly with the train of thought which the modern doctrine of progressive development has encouraged.

"'When animals,' he says, 'first crept forth from the newly formed earth, a dumb and filthy herd, they fought for acorns and lurking-places with their nails and fists, then with clubs, and at last with arms which, taught by experience, they had forged. They then invented names for things, and words to ex-press their thoughts, after which they began to desist from war, to fortify cities, and enact laws.' They who in later times have embraced a similar theory, have been led to it by no deference to the opinions of their pagan predecessors, but rather in spite of very strong prepossessions in favour of an opposite hypothesis, namely, that of the superiority of their original progenitors, of whom they believe themselves to be the corrupt and degenerate descendants.

" So far as they are guided by palæontology, they arrive at this result by an independent course of reasoning; but they have been conducted partly to the same goal as the ancients by ethnological considerations common to both, or by reflecting in what darkness the infancy of every nation is enveloped, and that true history and chronology are the creation as it were of yester-terday. Thus the first Olympiad is generally regarded as the earliest date on which we can rely, only 772 years before the Christian era." (P. 880.)

Here we are told that modern ethnologists have been led to entertain the idea that man existed at first in a barbarian state, partly " guided by palæontology," and partly by "ethnological considerations." The palæontological arguments we have already examined, and we flatter ourselves that we have proved them to be very far from possessing the force which has been ascribed to them. We now turn our attention to the other class of evidences, which he terms " ethnological."

He argues, in the first place, that darkness envelopes the infancy of every nation. He speaks of ethnologists having come to this conclusion in spite of " very strong prepossessions in favour of an opposite hypothesis, namely, that of the superiority of their original progenitors, of whom they believe themselves to be the corrupt and degenerate descendants." There is here a reference, that cannot be mistaken, to the belief of those who receive the history of our first parents, given by Moses, as an authentic narrative. When, therefore, he afterwards tells that the first Olympiad is the earliest date on which we can rely, he very plainly intimates that he regards the Old Testament as unworthy of credit. It would have been more consistent with his character as a fair and candid controversialist, if he had frankly and distinctly told us that he looked on the Hebrew Scriptures as destitute of authority; and—it would have been more in accordance with his fame as a philosopher, if he had stated his reasons for setting them aside.

If Sir Charles has any objections to bring against

the established belief of the Christian world, let him tell us what they are, and we will meet him with the boldness that befits us as Britons, and with the argument that becomes us as rational men.

We maintain, though some of our modern men of science may treat our statement with scorn, that there are other kinds of evidence besides those that geology finds in fossil remains; and that the belief which is placed by Jews and by Christians iu their sacred records rests upon proof of the most unquestionable kind, and that the more carefully they are scrutinised, and the more diligently the ancient history of nations is examined, the more fully is the truth of the Hebrew narratives confirmed. Before we can consent to set this record aside, we need arguments more weighty than quotations from Horace, or the groundless conjectures of modern savans. This record tells us that from the very beginning men were builders of cities, cultivators of the field, and artificers in brass and iron.

Even, however, if we were to allow that darkness covers the infancy of nations, and should agree to treat the testimony of Scripture as a thing of nought, we affirm that Sir Charles's opinion is untenable. The early history of the nations of modern Europe is not so far lost in the mist of ages, as to prevent us from learning that they owe the beginning of their civilization to Greece and Rome; and ancient annals, on which we can rely, tell us that Greece and Rome derived theirs from Syria and Egypt. History tells us of various barbarous tribes to whom the arts of life have been communicated by instructors from other lands. But there is not a single instance on record, in so far as we are aware, of any tribe rising from a barbarian state to one of civilization, through their own indigenous effort. We find many instances of national degradation, but not one of unaided, self-originating improvement. If this be true, then why should we attribute to the whole race that which cannot be affirmed of any one portion of it? The natural, the inevitable conclusion is, that if man in his primeval state had been a barbarian, and had been left to his own unaided resources, he would have been a barbarian still.

It is further affirmed, that if man had originally been placed in a state of civilization, he would have made much greater advancement in the arts of life than he has ever attained to:—

" The traditions of earlier ages, or of some higher and more educated caste, which has been destroyed, may have given rise to the notion of degeneracy from a primeval state of superior intelligence, or of science supernaturally communicated. But had the original stock of mankind been really endowed with such superior intellectual powers, and with inspired knowledge, and had possessed the same improvable nature as their posterity, the point of advancement which they would have reached ere this would have been immeasurably higher." (P. 378.)

In the first part of this quotation we find reference made to a higher and more educated caste, who are supposed to have been destroyed, and yet, in the latter part of it, we find the author reasoning as if advancement must necessarily be progressive! We have only to look to China and India to see how long civilization may remain stationary; to Assyria, Babylon, and Asia Minor, to see how far it may retrograde.

As to the "inspired knowledge" to which Sir Charles refers, we are constrained to ask, Has he ever read the record in which it is contained? Does he not know that it relates how man fell from "a primeval state of superior intelligence" through his own wilful transgression? Does he not know that the "science supernaturally communicated" has a direct and special reference to his spiritual and moral nature, and that it is only indirectly that it benefits his physical and intellectual condition? Does he not also learn from it, that though a rule be given from above, that rule cannot benefit those to whom it is revealed, unless they accept it as sent from God, and follow its counsels? He who wilfully closes his eyes, whether he be peasant or philosopher, must remain in darkness, though the brightest light that ever came from heaven should be shining around him.

At the time when our leading *savans* were vying with each other in their laudation of Sir Charles's volume, we were given to understand that it was altogether contrary to the rules of the British Association to make at its meetings any allusion to the statements of Scripture. But though the name of Moses may grate on the ears of some modern geologists, we retain our antiquated creed, and prefer the simple narrative of the Hebrew sage to the voluminous speculations of Sir Charles Lyell.

X.

FOSSIL HUMAN SKULLS.

THIS forms the subject of one of the most curious chapters in Sir Charles's work; and if we may judge from the number of engravings which he has given, and the trouble and expense he has bestowed on the inquiry, the subject must be one to which he attaches the highest importance. We concur with him in thinking the observations which he describes very interesting, though we suspect the conclusions which we draw from them are somewhat different from those which he contemplates.

Fossil Skull of the Engis Cave near Liége.—In a cavern at Engis, near Liége, a skull was found embedded in the same matrix with the remains of the elephant, rhinoceros, bear, hyæna, and other extinct animals. The skull was that of an adult individual. Dr Schmerling, who first directed attention to it, inferred, from the narrowness of the frontal portion, that it belonged to an individual of small intellectual development, and speculated on its Ethiopian characteristics; but when a cast was taken, and a more careful examination made, it was remarked that although the forehead was somewhat narrow, it might nevertheless be matched by the skulls of individuals of the European race. This observation has since been fully made out by measurement. Professor Huxley says that its height is good, and the forehead well arched, and that, on the whole, it exhibits a very fair development. Sir Charles concludes that it approaches near to the highest, or Caucasian, type.

Fossil Skull at Denise, in Central France.—At Denise a skull has been found, which geologists consider to have been coeval with the mammoth, and which is of the ordinary, or Caucasian, type.

Fossil Skulls in Denmark.—Skulls have been obtained, not only from peat, but from tumuli of the stone period, believed to be contemporary with the refuse mounds. These skulls are small and round, and have a prominent ridge over the orbits of the eyes, showing that the ancient race was of small stature, with round heads and overhanging eyebrows— in short, they bore a considerable resemblance to the modern Laplanders. Among them was one with a very low retreating forehead; but in general, judging from their form, they do not by any means indicate a race deficient in intellectual power.

Skull found at Meilen, on the Lake of Zurich.— Amid all the profusion of animal remains found in connection with the Swiss lake dwellings, extremely few bones of man have been discovered; and only one skull, dredged up from Meilen, on the Lake of Zurich, of the early stone period, seems as yet to have been carefully examined. Respecting this specimen, Pro-

F

fessor His observes, that it exhibits, instead of the small and rounded form proper to the Danish peat mosses, a type much more like that now prevailing in Switzerland, which is intermediate between the long headed and short headed form.

Skeleton of the Neanderthal Cave.—In 1857 a skeleton was found in a cave, situated in that part of the valley of the Dussel near Dusseldorf, which is called the Neanderthal. The cave occurs in the precipitous side of the winding ravine, about sixty feet above the stream, and a hundred feet from the top of the cliff. No bones of other animals were found along with it. When the skull and other parts of the skeleton were first exhibited, at a German scientific meeting at Bonn, some doubts were expressed by several naturalists whether it was truly human. Professor Schaaffhausen, who, with other experienced zoologists, did not share these doubts, observed that the cranium was of unusual size and thickness, the forehead narrow and very low, and the projection of the supra-orbital ridges enormously great. He also stated, that the absolute and relative length of the thigh bone, humerus, radius, and ulna, agreed well with the dimensions of a European individual of like stature at the present day; but that the thickness of the bones was very extraordinary, and the elevation and depression for the attachment of muscles were developed in an unusual degree. Some of the ribs, also, were of a singularly rounded shape and abrupt curvature, which was supposed to indicate great power in the thoracic muscles.

Professor Huxley says :—

" There can be no doubt that this skull is the most brutal of all known human skulls, resembling those of the apes, not only in the prodigious development of the superciliary prominences, and the forward extension of the orbits, but still more in the depressed form of the brain case, in the straightness of the squamose sutures, and in the complete retreat of the occiput forward and upward, from the superior occipital ridges.

" But the cranium in its present condition is stated to contain about 63 cubic inches of water. As the entire skull could hardly have held less than 12 cubic inches more, its minimum capacity may be estimated at 75 cubic inches. The most capacious healthy European skull yet measured had a capacity of 114 cubic inches ; the smallest about 55 inches, while some Hindoo skulls have as small a capacity as 46 cubic inches. The largest cranium of any gorilla yet measured contains 34·5 cubic inches. The Neanderthal cranium stands, therefore, in capacity very nearly on a level with the mean of the two human extremes, and very far above the pithecoid maximum.

" Hence, even in the absence of the bones of the arm and thigh, which, according to Professor Schaaffhausen, had the precise proportions found in man, although they were much stouter than ordinary human bones, there could be no reason for ascribing this cranium to anything but a man.

" The Neanderthal cranium has certainly not undergone compression, and in reply to the suggestion that the skull is that of an idiot, it may be urged that the *onus probandi* lies with those who adopt the hypothesis. Idiocy is compatible with very various forms and capacities of the cranium ; but I know of none which present the least resemblance to the Neanderthal skull."

This extraordinary skeleton has given rise to a great deal of discussion. In opposition to the opinion of Professor Huxley, a paper was read at Newcastle, in which an endeavour was made to show that it did not belong to the human family at all, and that it must be referred to a period antecedent to the appearance of man.

If we might hazard a conjecture, we would suggest the idea, that the very remarkable tendency to osseous development, shown in the uncommon strength of the other bones, and in the thickness of the skull, may in all probability have been the cause of the unusual form of the cranium; and we would further venture the supposition, that if, under the depressing influence of this bone-producing tendency, which prevented its expansion in the usual direction, the brain attained to a full average size, instead of conjecturing that the individual was an idiot, we should rather regard him as having been a man of more than ordinary energy of mind, as well as of uncommon bodily strength. Why may we not picture him to have been a zealous geologist, who, in his ardour to discover the conformation of the earth, explored the caverns of his district, till, meeting with some mephitic exhalation, he became a martyr to his scientific research?

So far as observation has as yet proceeded, the fossil human skulls of the European races may be considered as on an equality in point of development with those of the present inhabitants. They manifest a very decided superiority over those of the Australian, and other savage races of the present day.

Sir Charles gives us a variety of plates, by which we may be enabled to compare these ancient fossil

skulls with that of the modern European on the one
hand, and that of the Australian and chimpanzee on
the other. After examining his drawings and descriptions, we come to the conclusion that our civilization
has done but little to elevate the natural capacity of
the race, while a life of savage ignorance, like that of
the Australian, has done very much to degrade it.

This conclusion corresponds to that to which we
come when we consider the faculties and character
that are fitted for a state of civilization on the one
hand, and for a state of barbarism on the other. The
man in whom the higher faculties predominate, calm,
calculating, generous, sympathising, has the highest
prospect of usefulness in educated life. The man of
quick perception, low cunning, and brutal energy, is
better fitted for the precarious pursuits of the savage
state. A race possessing the highest European development, without the education, implements, and
arms, which social progress has supplied, would starve
with hunger if left to wander in the wilderness, while
the man of lower type would enjoy abundance. If
they engaged in war, the man of higher intellect would
speedily be subdued, while his enemies gained an easy
triumph.

The views we now express receive confirmation, if
we turn our attention to America. We there find
that the Ohian Toltecs, if we may judge of them by
their relics, were far superior in mental endowments
to the red races around them, by whom, however, they
seem to have been destroyed. Among the native

Americans, in more recent times, the Mandans used to be spoken of as exhibiting a talent and character so far superior to the tribes around them, that travellers spoke of them as belonging to a different race, and augured for them a high position in the future. They wanted, however, the low cunning and cruel ferocity of their neighbours, and by them they have been utterly exterminated.

We are thus led by a different line of argument to the same conclusion that we formerly expressed— If man's primeval state had been that of a barbarian, he would have remained a barbarian at the present day.

XI.

THE ORIGIN OF SPECIES BY VARIATION.

WHILE the primary and professed object of Sir Charles Lyell's volume is to adduce arguments in proof of the antiquity of man, the author has also in view, and, we are led to believe, has more especially in view, the giving his countenance and support to the theory of transmutation proposed by Mr Darwin in his work on the "Origin of Species."

The hypothesis advocated by Mr Darwin originated with some Continental writers, of whom Lamark and Oken are amongst the most distinguished. The account which they give of their views is more distinct than that of Mr Darwin:—

"Nature is not an intelligence, nor the Deity, but a delegated power,—an order of things instituted by the Supreme Being, and subject to certain fixed laws, which are the expression of His will. Nature proceeds gradually in all her operations, and cannot produce at once animals and plants of the higher classes, but must always begin by the formation of the most simple kinds, and out of them elaborates the more compound, adding successively different systems of organs, and multiplying, more and more, their number and their energy."— "By these means, not only is one species gradually changed into another, but genera and classes are themselves transformed; so

that there has been an uninterrupted succession in the animal
and vegetable kingdoms, from the earliest ages of the world, up to
the present day ; and the animals whose remains are discovered
in the strata of former epochs, however strange their forms may
appear, may nevertheless be regarded as the ancestors of those
now in existence."—" The race of mankind owe their peculiar
faculties to a similar cause."

This theory was afterwards made popularly known
in Britain by the anonymous author of the work entitled " The Vestiges of Creation." This work, char-
acterised by its pleasant style, the plausibility of some
of its arguments, and the amount of heterogeneous
information that it contained, attracted considerable
notice. A number of replies were published, some of
them by men of the highest eminence in literature and
science, and people imagined that no one would .ven-
ture again to maintain a hypothesis so refuted and con-
temned. A few years afterwards, however, Mr Darwin,
who had acquired considerable eminence as a naturalist,
published his volume on " The Origin of Species," in
which all the essential parts of Lamark's theory are
adopted. Professor Huxley then came forward, advo-
cating similar opinions. And now, Sir Charles Lyell
publishes his bulky volume, and lends the influence
of his name to their confirmation.

Mr Darwin's first proposition, if we may so term it,
is, that it is often difficult to determine the characteristics by which a species is distinguished from an
accidental variety. This he proves by a multitude of
illustrations. He also shows that, in some cases, the
hybrid offspring of different species are prolific. From

these data he infers that there is no real original distinction between species and genera, but that all are derived from the same source. He says :—

" I believe that animals have descended from at most only four or five progenitors, and plants from an equal or lesser number."—" I should infer from analogy, that probably all the organic beings which have ever lived on this earth, have descended from some one primordial form into which life was first breathed."

Sir Charles Lyell advocates the same opinions :—

" Every naturalist admits that there is a general tendency in plants and animals to vary, but it is usually taken for granted, though we have no means of proving the assumption to be true, that there are certain limits beyond which each species cannot pass, under any circumstances, or in any number of generations. Mr Darwin and Mr Wallace say that the opposite hypothesis, which assumes that every species is capable of varying indefinitely from its original type, is not a whit more arbitrary, and has this manifest claim to be preferred, that it will account for a multitude of phenomena which the ordinary theory is incapable of explaining."

To this specious reasoning we reply, that " the ordinary theory," as he terms it, is not, like that which he suggests, a mere conjecture, but a simple narrative of facts. Naturalists do not affirm that there are limits beyond which a species cannot pass under *any* circumstances, or in *any* number of generations. They simply state, as the result of their investigations, that there are certain limits which have never been passed, under any circumstances, or in any number of generations, that have come under the cognizance of man.

They have examined the records of creation, in many a lengthened page, and whether they direct attention to the organisms of the present timé, or to those that belong to the epochs of the past, they find that every species, when it first appears upon the terrestrial scene, has its organization perfect, and that it continues unchanged till its era has passed away. Some creatures seem to have lived upon earth for but a limited time; others have endured through lengthened ages, "for the four genera, Rhynconella, Crania, Discina, and Lingula, have been traced through the Silurian, Devonian, Carboniferous, Cretaceous, Tertiary, and Recent periods, and still retain in the existing seas the identical shape and character which they exhibited in the earliest formations." Whether their course upon earth has been long or short, naturalists tell us, that, after the most careful investigation they cannot trace in any species that gradual transformation of which Sir Charles speaks.

Mr Darwin's second proposition is, that the more delicate varieties of plants and animals, when left to carry on the struggle for existence, more especially in seasons of scarcity, will be overborne and finally exterminated by those whose growth is more vigorous, or whose peculiarities fit them for contending with the difficulties with which they are surrounded. This tendency of the more vigorous to supplant the feeble, he considers equivalent to a principle of natural selection, and conducts his argument on that supposition :—

" If we have under nature, variability, and a powerful agent
lways ready to act and to select, why should we doubt that
varieties in any way useful to beings, in their excessively complex relation of life, would be preserved, accumulated, and in-
herited ? As natural selection acts slowly, by accumulating
slight successive variations, it can produce no great or sudden
modifications. It can only act by very short and slow steps."

Sir Charles employs similar arguments :—

" A breeder finds that a new race of cattle, with short horns,
or without horns, may be formed in the course of several generations, by choosing varieties having the most stunted horns as
his stock from which to breed, so nature, by altering in the
course of ages the conditions of life, the geographical features
of a country, its climate, the associated plants and animals, and,
consequently, the food and enemies of a species, and its mode of
life, may be said by this means to select certain varieties best
adapted for the new state of things. Such new races may often
supplant the original type from which they have diverged,
although that type may have been perpetuated without modifi-
cation for countless anterior ages, in the same region, so long
as it was in harmony with the surrounding conditions then prevailing."

" Lamark, when speculating on the origin of the long neck of
the giraffe, imagined that quadruped to have stretched himself
up in order to reach the boughs of lofty trees, until by continued efforts, and longing to reach higher, he obtained an elongated neck. Mr Darwin and Mr Wallace simply suppose that,
in a season of scarcity, a long necked variety, having in this
respect the advantage over the rest of the herd, as being able to
browse on foliage out of their reach, survived them, and trans-
mitted its peculiarity of cervical conformation to its successors."

In replying to these speculations, we remark that,
in order to give any force to this reasoning, we must
suppose that the new varieties are possessed of a more

vigorous growth than the original species. But this is contrary to all experience. It is well known that varieties have, from time to time, been introduced; but these varieties, as a general, we may say as a universal rule, are less vigorous than those that resemble the parent stock; and it needs all the care of the cultivator and breeder to preserve them from extinction. Even the varieties themselves show an *atavism*, as naturalists term it, a tendency to return to the original form.

To show the fallacy of the transmutation theory, we have only to specify the assumptions that it requires us to make. In the first place, it requires us to believe that there have been epochs of enormous length, of which we have no memorial or evidence. In the next place, it requires us to believe that in these epochs a process of transmutation was continually going on of which we have no proof, and which must have been directly contrary to the system which has been pursued in the ages that are known.

We are told that the theory of natural selection " would explain the unity of type which runs through the whole organic world," would show the reason " why all living and extinct beings are united by complex lines of affinity with one another into one grand system," and " why there are distinct geographical provinces of species of animals and plants."

These are but conjectures and plausibilities, like those that occupied the attention of the schoolmen of the Middle Ages, and can end in nothing but vague speculation. If science is to continue that course which has led to such marvellous discoveries, it must discard unsupported conjecture, and confine attention to facts.

As to the origin of man, Mr Darwin's work seems especially intended to advocate the doctrine of Lamark, that, like all creatures here below, he has been produced by a slow system of transmutation from some simple organism of earlier epochs. The great object of his laborious research, the end and aim of his voluminous reasonings, is to prove that men are the natural descendants, the heirs, and lineal representatives of the limpet and the snail!

We cannot persuade ourselves that a man, who holds so high a rank among our men of science as that which Sir Charles Lyell is entitled to claim, can long continue to lend the sanction of his name in support of a theory so utterly destitute of authentic foundation, and so manifestly absurd in the conclusions to which it leads.

XII.

THE DIFFERENT VARIETIES OF THE HUMAN RACE.

THE difficulties with which a subject is beset, and the inadequacy of the means by which it may be elucidated, render the cautious inquirer anxious in his researches and hesitating as to his conclusions; while, on the contrary, they make the fanciful speculator reckless in his statements and arrogant in his assumptions. This remark has received abundant confirmation in the theories that have been proposed in regard to the origin of the different races of men, and in the dissertations that have appeared on the causes and means of their distribution over the earth. Among all these theories none is more curious than that of Sir Charles Lyell; and into it, as might be expected, the element of " ages " enters very largely.

In his former publication, to which in his present work he refers, he speculates on the causes that have led to the origin of races. In his recent publication he describes the means by which, as he supposes, they have been kept distinct. We direct attention, in the first place, to the statements which he makes in his " Principles of Geology," in regard to the causes

that have produced the different varieties of the
human race :—

"Naturalists have long felt that to render probable the received opinion, that all the leading varieties of the human family
have originally sprung from a single pair,—a doctrine against
which there appears to me to be no sound objection,—a much
greater lapse of time is required for the slow and gradual formation of races, such as the Caucasian, Mongolian, and Negro,
than is embraced in any of the popular systems of chronology.
The existence of two of the marked varieties above mentioned
can be traced back three thousand years before the present
time, or to the painting of pictures, preserved in the tombs, or
on the walls of buried temples, in Egypt. In these we see the
Negro and Caucasian physiognomies portrayed as faithfully,
and in as strong contrast, as if the likenesses of these races had
been taken yesterday. When we consider, therefore, the ex-
treme slowness of the changes which climate and other modifying causes have produced in modern times, we must allow for a
vast series of antecedent ages, in the course of which the long-
continued influence of similar external circumstances gave rise
to peculiarities, probably increased in many successive generations, until they were fixed by hereditary transmission."

The diversities found among the different races of
men are here ascribed to the effects of " climate and
other modifying causes," " producing changes with ex-
treme slowness." This assertion, however, manifestly
takes for granted the whole question under debate.
No proof is adduced in support of it, and various considerations show that it is altogether erroneous.

Whatever may have been the cause of the diversities that distinguished the different races of men,
Sir Charles's own statements are sufficient to show

that they do not proceed from the operation of slowly
acting causes. If, as he tells us, three thousand
years produce *no* change, welve housand would be
equally ineffective. Had he been able to trace a
gradually increasing diversity of form and feature in
the representations given of different nations, we
might have allowed his reasoning to be correct; but
if in pictures painted three thousand years ago, " we
behold the Negro and Caucasian physiognomies portrayed as faithfully, and in as strong contrast as if the
likenesses had been taken yesterday," we necessarily
conclude, that the peculiarities which distinguish them
must have originated in a totally different cause, and
that in no calculable amount of ages could the effect
of food and climate transform the Caucasian into the
Negro.

The following extract from his recent work, page
386, sets before us the means by which, as he conjectures, families were kept separate from one another,
while the various races were slowly acquiring their
different peculiarities :—

" So long as physiologists continued to believe that man had
not existed on the earth above six thousand years, they might
with good reason withhold their assent from the doctrine of a
unity of origin of so many distinct races ; but the difficulty becomes less and less, exactly as we enlarge our ideas of the lapse
of time during which different communities may have spread
slowly and become isolated, each exposed for ages to a peculiar
set of conditions, whether of temperature, or food, or danger,
or ways of living. The law of the geometrical rate of the increase of population, which causes it always to press hard on

the means of subsistence, would ensure the migration, in various directions, of offshoots from the society first formed abandoning the area where they had multiplied. But when they had gradually penetrated to remote regions by land or water,—drifted sometimes by storms and currents in canoes to unknown shores,—barriers of mountains, deserts, or seas, which oppose no obstacle to mutual intercourse between civilised nations, would ensure the complete isolation for tens or thousands of centuries of tribes in a primitive state of barbarism."

If there be any force in Sir Charles's arguments, we naturally conclude that the more widely separated races must exhibit the greatest diversity of figure and feature. Yet we find the Arabian and the Negro, living in circumstances precisely similar, and separated only by a narrow sea, exhibit the most remarkable diversity of development, while the Brahmin and the European, though they differ in colour, are closely allied in feature and form.

As to the barriers of mountains and deserts which are here spoken of as causing the complete isolation of tribes in a state of barbarism, they exist only in the writer's own imagination. There is no mountain or desert that could hinder the march of the roving barbarian; and if, as Sir Charles conjectures, the parents passed them in their outward migration, why could not the children repass them at an after time? His statements in regard to the barriers of seas can only refer to America and the scattered islands of the Pacific. They do not apply to the continents of the Old World, where, however, all the more remarkable varieties of the human race are found.

G

We remark again, that if men have been living upon the earth for "thousands of centuries," they must have left some evidence of that lengthened sojourn. Man in his most savage condition erects a dwelling, and makes use of weapons and tools. But we look in vain for the ruins of buildings, or the remains of art that periods so vast must necessarily have left behind them. In vain, too, do we search for the burying-places, the skeletons, or scattered bones of the unnumbered multitudes that, on such a supposition, must have lived and died on the earth.

The hypothesis of Sir Charles, in both its parts, in regard to the origin of the different varieties of the human race, and in reference to the means by which they have been kept distinct, in so far as we can perceive, is not supported by so much as a solitary fact, and has neither probability nor analogy to be adduced in its favour.

The difficulties that attend the theory we have been considering, have led some to adopt in preference that of M. Agassiz, who supposes that the diversity of the human species, found in different localities, may be most easily explained by supposing that mankind, instead of deriving their origin from a common parentage, have descended from a variety of original pairs created in the districts where their descendants still are found.

By adopting this hypothesis we, no doubt, escape the difficulties attending that which is advocated by Sir Charles Lyell. We must, however, remember, in

, the first place, that it is purely conjectural; and, in the next place, that it is directly opposed, not only to the Hebrew chronology, in support of which an array of evidence has been set forth which no reasonable man can lightly set aside, but, at the same time, to the early traditions of almost every nation. This last argument, in some of its more important particulars, is very beautifully illustrated by the late Mr Miller, in his " Testimony of the Rocks."

If we turn to Scripture for information in regard to the subject we are now considering, we find very little there that can help us in our inquiry into the origin of the diversities of form that are found among men. The Bible tells us of God's dealings with man as a moral and accountable being; it relates at length the means He employed in order to preserve among men a know-ledge of His character and of His law; but any in-formation in regard to the general affairs of the world, is only found in some incidental remark or passing allusion. When, therefore, we adduce a hypothesis of our own, which we think finds some confirmation in the Mosaic narrative, we trust that it will be kept in mind that we adduce it simply as a conjecture, which we bring forward with hesitation.

At the meeting at Newcastle we ventured to say that we should look on man, in reference to his bodily organization, as regulated by laws similar to those which have been assigned to the other creatures that people the globe, and that we will attain to the greatest probability in determining the question before us, if we have regard to the analogies that subsist throughout the whole organised creation.

No new distinctly marked variety of the human race has appeared for the last three thousand years, to show how such diversities have been produced; but varieties have occurred, both in the animal and vegetable kingdom, the history of which may assist us in our investigations.

When we direct attention to domesticated animals, for instance to the sheep, we find climate, food, and the care of the breeder, slowly producing changes; but these changes, though important to the sheep-master, affect only the comparative size of the animal, and the colour and length of its wool. No change is produced on its general characteristics, on its figure, or on the structure of its skeleton. There is, however, a variety of the animal in America that differs very widely from every other,—the legs of this very peculiar breed being so short and crooked, that the creature may be said to creep rather than to walk. This curious variety of the animal was not produced by a slow process of change continued through a long series of years. A farmer had a ewe which brought forth a lamb with the peculiarities to which we have referred. The idea struck him, that if a breed of such sheep could be raised, they would be much more easily kept within their enclosures than the ordinary kinds. The little deformed creature, therefore, was carefully tended. In the following season the ewe produced another lamb resembling the former one. These lambs, when they came to maturity, were kept separate from the rest of the flock, and in due time gave birth to offspring which inherit their parents' peculiarities. A permanent variety has thus been raised, not from the lengthened action of slowly operating causes, but from some inexplicable cause affecting the fœtal condition of their progenitors.

If we direct our inquiries into the vegetable kingdom, we find the changes that there take place originating in causes similar to those that prevail in the animated creation. There, we also remark, the field of observation is more extensive, inasmuch as varieties occur more frequently in the vegetable than in the animal world. In as far as we have been able to ascertain, all the more remarkable among these varieties have been produced by causes that affect the embryo condition of the seed, though the character of the variety may be preserved and intensified by the effects of cultivation.

Reasoning from analogy, therefore, we would say, that while the influence of a sultry climate may darken the complexion, and, in the course of a few generations, make the offspring of the Caucasian almost as black as the Negro, and while abundance of wholesome food, with proportionate exercise, may strengthen the muscles and increase the size of the human frame, the characteristics that distinguish the leading diversities of our race cannot have originated in the slowly acting effects of climate and food, but are rather to be regarded as the effect of some congenital influence that in a remote age affected the unborn child.

After stating these views at the meeting of the British Association, a gentleman present, who did not at all concur with us, gave the following curious confirmation of our argument:—

"Many years ago he met in Burmah a man covered all over with hair, and having no teeth. This man married a fair woman, and had two children, one of whom, a boy, was fair, and the other, a girl, was like her father, covered all over with hair, and had no teeth. When the girl grew up, some friends of his were anxious that she should marry, and accordingly they offered a large premium to any one who would take her for a wife. At length a man was found who was sufficiently courageous to do so. Two children were born of the marriage, and again one was fair, and the other the exact counterpart of its mother."

We observe, further, that these embryonic varieties, if we may so call them, seem to occur most frequently in animals when domesticated, and in plants when under cultivation,—in other words, when peculiarly favourable circumstances have induced an unusual vigour.

The Hebrew annals inform us, that in the early epochs of history man lived to a far greater age than he does now. This seems to imply a much more vigorous constitution than that which he at present possesses. They further tell us, that, while that vigour of constitution prevailed, remarkable varieties were produced. Both before and after the flood, it is said that " there were giants in those days." May we not, then, imagine, that the less remarkable, but more persistent varieties of our race, were in like manner produced, while the primeval vigour of the human constitution still continued?

As to the manner in which men were scattered over the face of the earth, and separated one from the other, we do not require to have recourse to hypotheses. We are told, that in order " to scatter them abroad upon the face of all the earth," the Lord " confounded their language, so that they might not understand one another's speech," and that by this means they were " divided in their lands, every one after his tongue, after their families, in their nations." The efficacy of such a means of separation needs no illustration.

If the conjecture we have ventured to suggest be admissible, the Scripture narrative leads us to conclude, that while the early vigour of our race still continued, and while its corresponding variety of bodily form was unimpaired by frequent intermarriage, the miraculous dispersion of mankind took place, and thus perpetuated the previously existing family peculiarities.

If our supposition be regarded as unwarrantable, and some other explanation be required, we are entitled to say, that if M. Agassiz gets out of the difficulties in which the origin of races is involved, by supposing the direct intervention of God in creating the different varieties, without having his philosophy called into question, those who believe in a record, in

which so many miracles are related, are warranted
in supposing, that when the Lord confounded the
language of men, in order yet more effectually to
separate them one from another, He gave them diversity of countenance and form, as well as diversity of
speech.

XIII.

ORIGIN AND DEVELOPMENT OF LANGUAGES AND SPECIES COMPARED.

Sir Charles has a chapter on this subject, to which we turned, in the hope that we would there find an account of the arguments which those who advocate the antiquity of man deduce from the history and phenomena of articulate speech. In this, however, we were disappointed. There is such a want of precision in his statements, that, after the most careful perusal, we were unable to discover anything, either in the facts which he brings forward, or in the reasoning which he employs, that has a distinct and immediate bearing either on the antiquity of man or on the origin of species.

We are, therefore, compelled to apply to another quarter for information, and are happy to find Mr Crawford, an active and influential member of the British Association, prepared to give us all the information we can desire.

This gentleman was President of the Geographical and Ethnological Section of the Association at its meeting at Manchester in 1861. On that occasion he gave the following succinct account of his views on the subject:—

" Among the many facts which attested the high antiquity of man was the formation of language. Language was not innate, but adventitious,—a mere acquirement, having its origin in the superiority of the human understanding. The prodigious num- ber of languages which existed was one proof that language was not innate,—some with a very narrow range of articulate sounds, others with a very wide one—some confined to single syllables, and others had many—some being very simple, and others of a complex structure,—thus implying that each tongue was a sepa- rate and distinct creation, or that each horde formed its own independent tongue. A whole nation might lose its original tongue, and in its stead adopt any foreign one. The language which was the vernacular one of the Jews three thousand years ago, had ceased to be so for above two thousand years ; and the descendants of those who spoke it were now speaking an infinity of foreign tongues, sometimes European, sometimes Asiatic. Languages derived from a single tongue of Italy had superseded the many native languages which were once spoken in Spain, in France, and in Italy itself. A language of German origin had nearly displaced, not only all the native languages of Britain and Ireland, but the numerous ones of a large portion of Ame- rica. Some eight millions of negroes were planted in the New World, whose forefathers spoke many African tongues, which tongues had nearly disappeared, having been supplanted by idioms derived from the German and Latin languages. It ne- cessarily followed that man, when he first appeared upon earth, was destitute of language."

We ask the reader to examine this extract, and see if he can trace any connection between the facts stated in the argument, and the conclusion to which the author comes. Does the great variety of languages now spoken upon earth, prove that man was originally destitute of speech? Do the many changes that language undergoes prove that at first there could have been none? Does the fact that the Jews now speak " an infinity of tongues," prove that their forefathers were dumb?

" Each separate tribe formed its own language, and there could be no doubt that in each case the framers were arrant savages, which was proved by the fact, that the rudest tribes ever discovered had already completed the task of forming a perfect language."

Here we are told, that because every tribe hitherto discovered has completed the task of forming a *perfect* language, there can be no doubt that, in each case, the framers were arrant savages. Are we then to understand, that if the language had been *imperfect,*.that would have shown the authors to have been philosophers and grammarians?

" The first rudiments of language must have consisted of a few articulate sounds, in the attempts made by the speechless but social savages to make their wants and wishes known to each other; and from these first efforts, to the time in which language had attained the completeness which they found it to have reached among the rudest tribes ever known to us, countless ages must be presumed to have elapsed. . . . . . The conclusion was inevitable, that the birth of man was of vast antiquity."

To this string of bold, unwarranted assertions and absurd conclusions, we need offer no reply. We set them before our readers as a specimen of the disquisitions that now go forth dignified by the name of Science.

These statements of Mr Crawford are copied from a published account of the proceedings of the meeting. A gentleman who was present has assured us of the accuracy of the report.

Such are the speculations to which, it seems, we must now turn for information in regard to the development of language and the early history of the human race. We must receive them with the respect that is due to the President of the Ethnological Section of the British Association. Moses speaks of a confusion of tongues at Babel, and the consequent dispersion of mankind. But who was Moses? The writings ascribed to him are a set of fables. Has not Sir Charles Lyell told us that authentic history is but of yesterday, and that the first Olympiad is the earliest date on which we can rely?

XIV.

THE AUTHOR OF NATURE.

THE strangest fallacy into which the advocates of the transmutation theory have fallen, is found in their reasoning with regard to the nature and work of the " Supreme Cause."

According to their view, the Deity, when first He formed the world, assigned certain laws to the creatures He had made, which are sufficient for the preservation of order and the perpetuation of life, amid all the variety of changes that can possibly take place. These laws, being sufficient for all emergencies, are absolutely unalterable, and the Deity intermeddles no more with the affairs of His creatures.

A miracle, that is, a departure in any circumstances from these unalterable laws, is of course a thing impossible; and, as an inevitable inference from this hypothesis, the work of redemption is a 'myth, and man's responsibility is a dream.

An independent, or direct act of creation, that is, the calling into being of a new species of animal or plant, is, like a miracle, inconsistent with the whole theory, and must consequently be rejected as undeserving of belief.

These doctrines, which are necessarily implied in the theory of transmutation, are advocated more or less distinctly by the different authors who have written in support of that hypothesis. While, therefore, we have no intention of making our little work a treatise on natural religion, our view of the speculations in which geologists have indulged would be incomplete, if we were to pass by without notice the statements which they have made in regard to the Author of nature.

Sir Charles Lyell.—The references to the great First Cause which we find in Sir Charles's last volume are but few. We give without abridgement his remarks on *Independent Creation :—*

" When I formerly advocated the doctrine, that species were primordial creations, and not derivative, I endeavoured to explain the manner of their geographical distribution, and the affinity of living forms to the fossil types nearest akin to them in the tertiary strata of the same part of the globe, by supposing that the creative power which originally adapts certain types to aquatic, and others to terrestrial conditions, has, at successive geological epochs, introduced new forms best suited to each area and climate, so as to fill the places of those which may have died out."

With this view of independent creation we concur, only remarking, that we dislike the term " creative power," as it seems to imply something distinct from the living, intelligent, and ever-present God, to whom reason teaches us to look as the Author and Preserver of all.

" In that case, although the new species would differ from the old (for these would not be revived, having been already proved, by the fact of their extinction, to be incapable of holding their ground), still they would resemble their predecessors generically. For, as Mr Darwin states in regard to new races, those of a dominant type inherit the advantages which made their parent species flourish in the same country, and they likewise partake in those general advantages which made the genus to which this parent species belonged a large genus in its own country.

" We might, therefore, by parity of reasoning, have anticipated that the creative power, adapting the new types to the new combinations of organic and inorganic conditions of a given region, such as its soil, climate, and inhabitants, would introduce new modifications of the old types,—marsupials, for example, in Australia, new sloths and armadilloes in South America, new heaths at the Cape, new roses in the Northern, and new camelias in the Southern hemisphere."

With these speculations we are not by any means prepared to agree. That every creature is prepared for its destined habitation, we look on as one of the best established proofs of the infinite wisdom of Him who rules creation ; but we do not conclude that the only reason by which the Author of nature is guided in His procedure, is the adaptation of the individual creature to the locality it is destined to occupy—a higher object is the harmony and general good of the whole ; and there may be many other reasons, beyond the range of human observation, and beyond the reach of human understanding.

" But to this line of argument Mr Darwin and Dr Hooker reply, that when animals or plants migrate into new countries, whether assisted by man, or without his aid, the most successful colonisers appertain by no means to those types which are most allied to the old indigenous species. On the contrary, it more frequently happens, that members of genera, orders, and even classes, distinct and foreign to the invaded country, make their way most rapidly, and become dominant, at the expense of the endemic species. Such is the case with the placental quadrupeds in Australia, and with horses and many foreign plants in the Pampas of South America, and numberless instances in the United States, and elsewhere, which might easily be enumerated. Hence the transmutationists infer, that the reason why these foreign types, so peculiarly fitted for these regions, have never before been developed there, is simply that they were excluded by natural barriers. But these barriers of sea, or desert, or mountain, could never have been of the least avail, had the creative force acted independently of material laws, or had it not pleased the Author of nature that the origin of new species should be governed by some secondary causes, analogous to those which we see preside over the appearance of new varieties, which never appear except as the offspring of a parent stock, very closely resembling them."

This extract affords a characteristic instance of the transmutationist style of argument. We have, in the first place, a partial statement of facts. Plants and animals recently introduced into various parts of the world, have in many instances taken the place of those that were indigenous; but it does not follow that if left alone they would continue during the course of many generations to maintain their supremacy. Every cultivator of the soil, farmer or gardener, knows that "a change of seed"—the sowing of seed grown in a different locality—produces a more luxuriant crop than could be raised from seed got in the immediate vicinity; but this advantage continues only for a season or two. In like manner, there is reason to suspect

that European animals and plants, transported to dis-
tant realms, may in the course of generations lose their
present vigour. ·

In the next place, we have reasons and objects
assigned to the Author of nature which are altogether
unwarranted. They tell us, that "the reason why
these foreign types, so peculiarly fitted for these regions, have never been developed there, is simply that
they were excluded by natural barriers." No counsel
or intelligent choice is left to the Creator. Those who
believe in the existence of an almighty and benevolent God, who does not confine His view to the in-
terests of some one individual creature, but has regard
to the good of the whole, may be led to entertain the
opinion, that these creatures were excluded because
their vigorous growth and corresponding˙ strength
would have proved destructive to other creatures of
less vigorous constitution, but equally entitled to the
Creator's care. Mr Darwin's theory excludes the
idea of any regard having been paid to benevolent design, in introducing new creatures into the terrestrial
scene. His whole argument proceeds on the supposition that the "law of the strongest," in all circumstances, regulates the course of creation. We do not
agree with him ; and we hold that it is far better that,
in the natural world, as well as in the moral govern-
ment of man, a more merciful rule should be followed.
The evidences of benevolent design which we see in
all the Creator's arrangements with regard to sentient
beings lead us to conclude, that His great object is

H

"the greatest good of the greatest number." For such an object the transmutation theory makes no provision. According to the description given of it by its supporters, the law of development is as hard and unfeeling in its character, as the arguments adduced in favour of it are unwarranted and absurd.

In another part of the volume Sir Charles refers again to the law of development :—

" In our attempts to account for the origin of species, we find ourselves still sooner brought face to face with the working of a law of development, of so high an order, as to stand nearly in the same relation as the Deity himself to man's finite understanding—a law capable of adding new and powerful causes, such as the moral and intellectual faculties of the human race, to a system of nature, which had gone on for millions of years without the intervention of any analogous cause. If we confound 'variation' or 'natural selection' with such creational laws, we deify secondary causes, or immeasurably exaggerate their influence."

In this quotation, which we frankly acknowledge that we do not understand, Sir Charles speaks of "deifying secondary causes." By a secondary cause we understand certain properties imparted by God to His creatures, from which definite effects or consequences proceed. The law of development is not a secondary cause. It has no real existence. In attributing to it the powers and offices which they assign, the transmutationists ascribe the perfections of the Deity to an idle dream, and give the homage and honour which are due to the great Author of all to a creature of their own imagination.

Mr Darwin.—In our remarks on the extracts which we have just considered, we have already directed attention to the views of Mr Darwin. There is, therefore, no reason why we should again refer to them.

It is right, however, to observe, that these two gentlemen do not appear altogether to correspond in opinion. Sir Charles brings forward the arguments against "independent creation" with a measure of reserve and hesitation, which seems to imply a longing regard for his former belief. Mr Darwin, on the contrary, expresses the most triumphant confidence in the incontrovertible accuracy of his conclusions :—

" Authors of the highest eminence seem to be fully satisfied with the view that each species has been independently created.

" To my mind, it accords with what we know of the laws impressed on matter by the Creator, that the production and extinction of the past and present inhabitants of the world should have been due to secondary causes, like those determining the birth and death of the individual. . . . . .

" These authors seem no more startled at a miraculous act of creation than at an ordinary birth. But do they really believe that, at innumerable periods in the earth's history, certain elemental atoms have been commanded suddenly to flash into living species? The day will come when this will be given as a curious illustration of the blindness of preconceived opinion."

The Author of " The Vestiges of Creation."—The leading doctrines of the transmutationists in reference to the Author of nature, as we before stated, are, that the Deity does not act directly in preserving and regulating His creatures, but employs the law of development as an intermediate agent, in carrying on His work. To this agent, as shown by the last extract from Sir Charles.Lyell, they ascribe the office, and, it would appear, the attributes, of Deity. At the same time this agent has no liberty of action, but is bound by regulations more stern than those which the ancients ascribed to the Fates. They further hold, that the great Supreme, having made these arrangements, interferes no more in the concerns of His creatures. In support of these views, which Sir Charles adopts, though with some little hesitation, and which Mr Darwin confidently proclaims, the author of the " Vestiges " endeavours to reason ! He says :—

" It must further be recollected, that we are not only to account for the origination of organic being upon this little planet, third of a series, which is but one of hundreds of thousands. We have to suppose that every one of these numerous globes is either a theatre of organic being, or in the way of becoming so. Is it conceivable, as a fitting mode of exercise for creative intelligence, that it should be paying a special attention to the creation of species, as they may be required in each situation throughout these worlds, at particular times? Is such an idea accordant with our general conception of the dignity, not to speak of the power, of the great Author? Yet such is the notion which we must form if we adhere to the doctrine of special exercise."

These arguments, and the whole of the transmutationist theory, in so far as it has reference to the Supreme Being, rest on an utterly mistaken idea of the character and perfections of the Deity. They proceed from those who entertain them ascribing views and feelings to the Creator which are only appropriate to man.

If we look to the starry firmament, and examine into the wonders which the telescope reveals, we see at a glance that there is nothing too great for the power and wisdom of Deity to accomplish and to sustain. If we consider the arrangements made for the existence and happiness of animated beings, and direct our attention to the mysteries of the world of animalcules, displayed by the microscope, we find that there is nothing so small as to escape His observation, nothing so insignificant as to be unworthy of His benevolent regard. If this be the case, how futile are the arguments we have quoted ?

" Is it," says the author, " a fitting mode of exercise for creative intelligence, that it should be paying a special attention to the creation of species, as they may be required in each situation throughout these worlds ?" We unhesitatingly answer that it is. When *a man* has committed to his charge duties of importance, we consider him as acting a very inconsistent part if he occupies his thoughts with a multitude of trifling details. The reason is obvious. Our minds are so constituted, that a close attention to minute particulars unfits us for paying a due regard to more important matters. A great variety of objects distracts us, and, therefore, our wisdom consists in selecting that one pursuit which is more especially deserving of regard, and making it our peculiar care; while other things of less interest are either altogether postponed, or receive but little regard. There is, however, a wide difference between the method of procedure that is appropriate to the capacities of man, and that which is appropriate to the attributes of *God.* No multiplicity of detail can perplex the mind of Him who is infinite in wisdom, and no amount of labour can burden Him who is almighty in power.

It is because our capacity is limited that we must neglect minutiæ and confine our care to more important concerns, lest by attempting too much we do nothing well. It is for the same reason that we are constrained to employ agents in carrying on our labours. The multitude of his servants is only a proof that the master's ambition exceeds his own natural powers. The instruments and agents employed by man are all evidences of his weakness. He employs them because he cannot accomplish his purposes without them.

On the other hand, He who is infinite in wisdom and power can attend to all things, whether great or small, without feeling either perplexity or fatigue. He asks no counsel, and He needs no assistance. Everywhere present throughout the wide expanse of space, He manifests the infinitude of His attributes and the perfection of His nature, by acting everywhere; and by acting everywhere directly and alone.

It has been asked, " Is it suited to the dignity of the great Supreme, to suppose that He is continually watching over the insect world, and to believe that the size and form, the limbs and members, of every

animalcule, are all the objects of His peculiar care?"
Again we reply in the affirmative. The great Creator
cares even for the meanest of the beings He has formed.
He adapts the various limbs and members, appetites
and habits, of the microscopic insect, to the sphere
which it is destined to fill, in the same manner, and
for the same reason, that He has fitted man for the
world which he inhabits,—in the same manner, and
for the same reason, that He has filled the universe
with the creatures it contains. He does it by the
word of His power, and for the purpose of enabling
His creatures to enjoy the life which He bestows.

Our ideas of dignity and importance are all comparative. We look on the filling of the tiny stagnant
pool with its multitude of infusorial creatures as a
matter of very little moment; we regard the peopling
of a world as a very mighty work; because in relation
to the pool man is great, and in relation to the world
he is small and insignificant. We must not, however,
ascribe our ideas of greatness and importance to God.
All creatures are alike, when they are compared to
Him. The angel and the worm are equally insignificant when brought into comparison with Him that
made them. If, on the one hand, there is no work so
complicated as to perplex His counsels, and no task
so difficult as to exhaust His energies or cause Him to
feel fatigue; on the other hand, there is nothing so
small as to escape His notice, or be unworthy of His
care.

In like manner, difficulty and ease are terms appro-

priate to man, and to other creatures whose strength
and skill are limited; but they are not appropriate to
the Almighty God.   It is as easy for Him who is infinite, to people a universe, as it is to fill a shell.   He
speaks the creating word, and the tiny insect creeps
from under the clod; and He does but speak again,
when legions of angels start into being, arrayed in
glory, and hymning their Maker's praise.   He commands, and creation obeys.   He wills, and it is done.

Throughout the whole expanse of space to which
our knowledge extends, we see a harmony of arrangement and a uniformity of design which plainly indicate the all-pervading counsel and continuous activity
of a *master mind.*   At the same time, we find in every
creature, however minute, the evidence of such ex-
quisite skill and perfection of finish, as clearly de-
monstrates the elaborate workmanship, if we may so
express ourselves, of a *master hand.*   All the orbs of
heaven are upheld by His power, and all the things
they contain are guided by His law.   At the same
time, He lavishes on the smallest and meanest of His
creatures the same unremitted attention, the same
unwearied and unceasing solicitude that He would
have shown had it formed the whole of His work.
He bestows on every one of the unnumbered insects
that creep on the earth, the same regard that He
would have paid to it had it stood alone, and been
the undivided object of His care—the whole of His
creation.

He sustains and regulates every event, whether great

or small; but the burden of the universe does not oppress Him. He employs no intermediate agent—because He needs no help. And He seeks no rest—because He needs no repose. " The everlasting God, the Lord, the Creator of the ends of the earth, fainteth not, neither is weary."

XV.

MAN'S PLACE IN CREATION.

IN the concluding part of his volume Sir Charles gives us disquisitions on the osteology of the different divisions of the human family, as compared with that of the ape; dissertations on the anatomical structure of the brain in man and in other animals; and a variety of extracts from authors who have written on the mental and psychological constitution of our race. Though the scope of his argument is not always very perspicuous, the whole is evidently brought forward in support of that part of the Darwinian theory which refers to the nature of man, and to the place which he occupies in the animated creation.

The questions to be inquired into are more abstruse than those which have hitherto occupied our attention, and cannot be satisfactorily determined, without a much more extended discussion than is consistent with the plan of our present work. As a reply, however, to the speculations brought forward in the " Antiquity of Man " would be incomplete without some notice of this part of the work, we shall give a brief account of our views on the subject, and refer any reader desirous of a more detailed explanation, to a work which we formerly published on the "Rational Creation." This part of his work, moreover, more especially demands a reply, inasmuch as it is directly opposed not only to the tenets of inspiration, but to the fundamental doctrines of natural religion.

THE BODILY ORGANIZATION OF MAN.—That the material frame of man in many respects resembles that of the ape, and that in other particulars it is very different, is evident even to the most careless observer. We do not require any elaborate anatomical disquisition to prove that the lower extremities of man are better fitted than those of the ape for standing or walking in an upright position, and that his hands are better adapted for holding and employing implements of art.

It appears to us that no great importance needs be attached to the discussions that have arisen as to the place which his superior organization entitles man to hold in the classification of the naturalist. Whether the order Bimana should be separated from that of the Quadrumana does not seem a question of great moment. We are inclined to think that, judging simply from the peculiarities of his bodily frame, man is entitled to be reckoned in a class by himself; but if others think that he is more appropriately placed at the head of the apes, we are willing to allow that "something may be said on both sides." It matters little what rank may be assigned to him, when our arrangements are merely guided by his bodily form. The great, the only essential distinction between him and the other creatures here below, is found in those characteristics which show him to be possessed of the powers and aspirations of a rational and immortal being. We fully concur with the words of the poet :—

"A man is measured by his soul."

ANIMAL FACULTIES AND DESIRES IN MAN.—All writers on mental phenomena, and, we may add, all who have ever thought of the subject, agree in dividing the properties of the mind into two classes, the Faculties and the Desires. The first includes the various powers by which we are enabled to perceive, remember, and determine. The second includes the different appetites and emotions that excite the activity both of body and of mind. As it would be altogether foreign to our present purpose to enter into a detailed examination of this subject, we consider it sufficient to make a few brief observations on the different classes into which these powers and feelings may be divided.

The Primary Faculties.—These take cognizance of the information conveyed to the mind, by the senses of sight, hearing, smelling, taste, and touch. They have associated with them corresponding affections, by which we are led to take pleasure in the exercise of these powers. Hunger, thirst, the love of life, and some other feelings, may be regarded as belonging to the same class. All these faculties and desires are found in the lower orders of animals as well as in man, and, generally speaking, have a more important office assigned to them in the lower types of existence than they have in the human race.

The Perceptive Faculties.—These powers might with some propriety be called the internal senses,—each one having assigned to it a particular object, which it perceives, and in respect to which it forms its determinations, in the same manner as the eye perceives the rays of light, and judges of their intensity and their hue. Among them we reckon memory, by which we store up the intelligence brought to us by the other faculties, and bring it forward again at an after time when circumstances require; along with it we may mention those powers by which we judge of position, duration, succession, order, number, and quantity. These primary faculties hold a kind of middle place between those that take cognizance of the sensations communicated by the external senses, and the reflective powers which yet remain to be mentioned. When they predominate in any person, they communicate to him the character of readiness and quick observation. Their deficiency produces that simplicity and absence of mind which are sometimes found in persons in other respects distinguished for talent even of the highest order. All are agreed that these faculties are common to man, and to the higher orders of the irrational creatures.

The Reflective Faculties are those by which we are enabled to trace the relation between cause and effect; to judge of resemblances, distinctions, and contrasts, and to contrive, or determine on the means best adapted for accomplishing an end. These faculties belong to a higher order than those which we before enumerated. They are directed to subjects of a more abstruse and recondite kind. They classify and arrange the information we have received, which without such arrangement would only be a mass of lumber; and they enable us to apply it to practice, without which our observations would be of no avail.

Sentiments and Affections.—Besides the appetites and desires connected with the bodily senses, we have a variety of feelings, to which we usually give the names of sentiments and affections. They may be arranged into three classes : the intellectual emotions, such as the love of knowledge, the love of imitation, the love of the new and marvellous, the love of the sublime and the beautiful, and the love of the ludicrous; the sentiments, such as sympathy, reverence, pity, firmness, self-esteem, love of approbation, cautiousness, and hope; and the affections, by which we are led to take pleasure in the company of our friends, our families, and our fellow-men.

The list which we have here given of the animal faculties and desires includes some which are commonly regarded as peculiar to man. The reflective faculties, and some of the higher emotions, for instance, have been spoken of as if the possession of them constituted the chief distinction between the mind of man and the spirit of the beast. But after the most careful investigation of the subject, we have come to the conclusion that they all belong, in a greater or less degree, to various classes of irrational beings. In these creatures we do not find the power of tracing the connec-

tion between cause and effect, or the contriving faculty
by which we adapt means to an end, so fully developed
as they are in man ; but the manifold instances of con-
trivance and design which are continually exhibited,
not only by birds and beasts, but even by insects,
prove that these faculties are found, though in a more
limited degree, even in them.   It is a much more
difficult task to determine in how far the lower orders
of creation are possessed of the intellectual emotions
and higher sentiments.   The ape and monkey afford
abundant evidence of their being susceptible of the
emotion of imitation; the spaniel, crouching at the
foot of his master, and licking his hand, shows that
he can be influenced by reverence for superior power.
The determination with which almost every creature
defends its own habitation from the intrusion of a
stranger, the punishment inflicted by the citizens of
the rookery on those offenders that have been detected
in the act of plundering, and other facts of a similar
kind, show that animals have an idea of property, and
a sense of justice.   We are inclined to think that the
lower creatures may be described as possessing all of
these emotions, though in a degree far inferior to that
in which they are found in man.

In regard to the doctrine of the phrenologists, who
maintain that there is a correspondence between the
powers and feelings of the mind and particular portions
of the brain, all that can as yet be asserted with confidence is, that the brain seems to be that part of the
human frame on which the mind primarily exerts its

influence. All the nerves, by means of which we gather in our information with respect to the external world, terminate there. Any disease or injury of the brain affects the mind more immediately than a similar disease or injury in any other part; while a deficiency in the general size of the brain indicates corresponding imbecility of mind. The whole science of the phrenologist, in as far as it can in any sense be regarded as established, amounts only to this, that particular portions of the brain are the organs of particular faculties and emotions, and that the comparative size of these organs may be regarded as an index pointing out the predominating powers and feelings. A forehead, for example, projecting in the lower part, and sloping rapidly above, is an indication of the predominance of the perceptive faculties; while a full development of the upper portion may be regarded as a sign that the reflective powers prevail. The charge of materialism that has been brought against these views we consider altogether unfounded. Even allowing that there is a constant correspondence between the strength of particular faculties and emotions and the corresponding portions of the brain, it does not follow that the feelings and faculties are dependent on the organs. On the contrary, analogy leads us to conclude, that as the mind is the more important part of the man, the material instrument is made to correspond to the faculty that acts upon it; that the workman is not made for the sake of the instrument, but the instrument for the use of the workman.

Thus far the opinions advocated by the transmutationists do not differ essentially from our own. But here the correspondence between us ends. They hold that the faculties and feelings which we have enumerated constitute the whole of the mental characteristics of man; we hold that, in addition to the powers and affections which he has in common with the irrational creatures, he is possessed of others of a totally different and far more exalted kind.

To that nobler part of man we now direct attention, deeply regretting that we are not able to do that justice to the subject which its importance demands.

THE SOUL OF MAN.—Some writers, who have published treatises on the science of mind, take no notice of the mental peculiarities by which man is distinguished from the other inhabitants of the earth. Some seem to think, that the only distinction between the faculties of man and those of the beast consists in the superior strength and activity which these faculties manifest in the human race. Others, as we before remarked, enumerate certain powers and emotions, which they say are peculiar to man; but these powers are represented as precisely similar in character to those that are found in other creatures, and consequently, on this supposition, all animals here below are essentially the same in their nature, and man only differs from the others in being more largely endowed. The inquiries which we have made have brought us to a very different conclusion. We regard the soul of man as altogether different, both in its nature and in

I

its destiny, from the spirit that animates the beast.
In addition to the material frame which he possesses
in common with every other member of the organic
creation, and to the living principle, with its corresponding faculties and feelings, by which he is distinguished from the herb and tree and allied to the
animated tribes, he has a soul, a rational spirit, altogether distinct from anything found in the other races
of earth-born beings, the possession of which renders
him as much superior to the lower animals as they are
superior to the plant, and as the plant is superior to
the stone.

Reason.—The primary faculty by which the soul of
man is distinguished from mere animal intelligence,
and the understanding of man from the sagacity of
the brute, is the power by which we form an idea of a
quality or attribute as something distinct and separate
from the object in which it resides.

This faculty enables us to attach a meaning to such,
terms as whiteness and hardness, without having. before our minds any particular object in which the properties are found. It enables us to form an intelligent
notion of sentiments and emotions, such as hatred and
love, without our having any immediate reference to
the objects that awaken these emotions, or to the
effects which they produce. It compares together the
various facts brought under its notice by the animal
faculties and senses ; it decides upon their nature, and
classifies circumstances, persons, and things, according
to the qualities which they exhibit. It observes the

working of emotions and affections, and judges of the character of actions, by tracing them to the motives from which they proceed. It takes cognizance, in short, of essential properties and abstract relations.

It was Locke, we believe, who first employed the term abstraction to denote this more simple and ordinary operation of the reasoning power; when, like the chemist, who extracts from the various herbs employed in medicine the essences in which their virtue consists, and who thereby enables the physician to preserve them uninjured, and to apply them with effect, it deduces general principles from observation and experiment, and draws practical lessons for the guidance of our conduct from the multitudinous occurrences with which memory is stored.

Reflection, in its more appropriate signification, denotes the effort by which the mind, having collected together a variety of similar facts, deduces from an examination of their properties some general principle, which constitutes the original cause of their characteristic and distinctive peculiarity. It infers the nature of general causes from a comparison and induction of particular results.

By what we may call a reverse operation of the same faculty, from an acquaintance with the nature and effects of these general causes, we determine the probable consequences that will result if they be brought into operation in any given conjuncture.

This power of abstraction imparts a peculiar character to the operations of the rational mind. The lower

creatures have their attention aroused by present sen-
sation, or by remembrance of external occurrences.
Man has the faculty of turning his thoughts to whatever objects he may desire to investigate, whether they
be present before his senses, or shrouded in the re-
cesses of the past, or hidden in the remotest obscurities
of the future. He can do more; in the exercise of
what is usually termed imagination, he can group
together ideas selected at pleasure from those which
memory supplies, and he can clothe, as it were, one
object with the qualities that belong to another, and
thus form new and ideal combinations.

As it is only through the exercise of the inferior
faculties and senses that the rational soul can acquire
any knowledge of that which is external to itself, and
only through them that it can hold communication
with others, it is difficult in a great many mental phenomena to draw a line of distinction between that
which is to be ascribed to the agent, and that which
is due to the instruments employed. It is, consequently, almost impossible to describe with precision
the functions that belong to the reasoning power of
the soul. But it is very evident, when we compare it
with the perceptive and reflective powers, which we
formerly described, that we must look on it as standing alone. It is not one of a multitude, *par inter pares.*
It is not one of a company, equal in influence and
similar in nature. Its office is peculiar, and its influence is supreme. It is the builder by whom the
edifice of demonstration is erected; the other faculties

are merely the labourers that bring in the materials. It is the general that directs the onward march of argument; the others are merely the scouts that bring in intelligence, the messengers that convey his orders, and the subordinates that execute his commands.

Language.—There is probably no distinction between the rational and the irrational creation that so readily attracts the attention of the casual observer, as the faculty of speech in man and the want of it in other creatures. Some authors have spoken of the various signs and inarticulate cries by which animals communicate to each other their intentions and feelings, as being of the same nature as the speech of man; but a very brief examination of what has been called the language of beasts will be sufficient to show the wide difference that exists between it and the language of man. The sounds uttered by animals are merely the instinctive expressions by which they make known the desires and sensations which they experience at the time. When the dog, for example, finds himself in want, whether he is hungry and requires food, or in confinement and wishes for freedom, he gives expression to his feelings by whining and howling; when he is irritated, he shows his anger by snarling and growling; when he is frightened, or in pain, he expresses his apprehension or suffering by yelping; and when startled by a stranger's approach, he shows his alarm by barking. The utterance of these sounds awakens sympathy, more especially in other animals of the same species, and may thus enable him to obtain the end he desires. All his varied notes—and there is none of the lower creatures that possesses so extensive a vocabulary—only express present sensations, and beyond this his language does not go. The same remark may be made in regard to all the signs and sounds that are made use of by the various tribes of irrational creatures.

The language of man is based on an altogether different principle. It is intended to point out the character and qualities of the persons and objects to which we refer. The first lisping attempts of the child evidence a desire to describe the things that please him as " good," and the things that displease him as " bad." When we think, we discriminate qualities, we classify and arrange them; and language is the expression of the thoughts, or conclusions, to which we come. In speech, we communicate to others the opinions we have formed of the character and qualities of the objects around us.

That this is the nature of human discourse, may be shown by tracing out the original meaning of the words in common use. Grammarians tell us that there are eight or nine different classes of words, or parts of speech, as they are usually termed; but of these, one half—the adverb, preposition, interjection, and conjunction—are but abbreviated forms of the others. The conjunction *if*, for example, is a corruption of *gif*, the old imperative of the verb to *give*. The adverbs *when* and *while* are nouns, denoting a space of time, of which *while* is still employed as a noun, though *when* in that acceptation has become obsolete. Those who wish to see this inquiry carried out to its full extent, may consult Horne Tooke's "Diversions of Purley," in which the statement we have made is fully demonstrated. Two of the remaining parts of speech, the article and the pronoun, we find no difficulty in referring to the adjective and noun. Words are thus found to consist of three general divisions,—the adjective, the verb, and the noun; and these, on further examination, may all be classed under the definition usually given of an adjective—" a word that denotes some quality or circumstance." The verb is described as denoting either action or the endurance of an action. The performing of an action, and the enduring of an action, are merely two different classes of "qualities;" and the relationships of time and dependence, which constitute the distinction between tenses and moods, are merely "circumstances" connected with them. The substantive or noun is said to be the name of a thing; but what is meant by a *name?* Often, no doubt, in modern speech, the noun is a mere arbitrary sound, employed by common consent to designate some particular person, place, or thing, without any meaning being suggested by the word itself; but originally all names are significant, and denote some particular quality or circumstance which distinguishes the individual they are employed to designate. The original meaning of many of the substantives that are found in the English language is now forgotten, but in regard to a great part of them it can still be traced, and these all point out

properties and circumstances. All the nouns that have
of late been added to our language denote qualities.
We may mention, for example, *umbrella*, a little shade;
telescope, that which perfects vision; *thermometer*, a
measurer of heat. All the new terms employed in
every department of art or philosophy, are, in like
manner, significant of properties and circumstances.
It thus appears that words are arbitrary signs denoting
qualities; and language is the communicating of information with regard to the qualities, or qualifying
circumstances, that distinguish the objects which form
the subject of our discourse. The language of beasts,
as was before observed, is altogether different. It consists of the natural and instinctive sounds by which
they express present sensations, and has nothing corresponding to it in the speech of man, excepting a few
of our interjections.

Barter, Trade, and Use of Money.—Dr Adam Smith
speaks of the circumstance of brutes having no idea of
the interchange of property, as constituting an essential difference between .them and man, and remarks,
that no one ever saw one dog barter a bone with another. Some authors have opposed this opinion, and
speak of the aid given to each other by animals labour-
ing in concert, as a proof that they have a very distinct idea of mutual agreement. We observe, however, that mutual agreement and conjoint labour do
not imply any abstract ideas, which barter, and more
especially the use of money, and other arbitrary signs
denoting property, evidently do. To these things,

therefore, we refer, with Dr Smith, as a proof of an essential distinction between man and the lower orders of creation.

Capacity and Desire for Improvement.—That power, of whîch abstraction and reflection are the operations, and which is manifested in the use of language and employment of money, has yet another peculiarity to which we must advert. It is capable of indefinite advancement, and there is a corresponding pleasure taken in its continual increase.

Not only do we find the store of knowledge possessed by each individual capable of great enlargement, but the amount of information accumulated by the human race, as a whole, is receiving daily accessions, and we can assign no limit to its increase. Every new discovery in art and science, whether it be the result of casual observation, or of protracted study, enlarges the field of knowledge, and increases our powers of research ; and what the result of future discoveries may be, no one can venture to anticipate.

This capacity for unlimited improvement, and more especially this desire for onward progress in knowledge, forms not only a marked difference between man and the lower orders of creation, but presents a decided contrast to their limited powers and yet more limited inclinations. The inferior animals inherit not only the capacities of their parents, but in a great measure the knowledge which their parents acquire, and, consequently, attain to very great perfection in the circumscribed range of intellectual exertion to which their faculties and necessities confine them; but beyond that range they do not pass. No architect could build a nest more suitable for the purposes required, than that which the bird constructs for herself; no mechanician could form a honey-comb more mathematically accurate in all its dimensions, than that which the insect fabricates; but there is no onward progress in their art. Centuries pass on, and birds and bees continue to build as birds and bees have built before.

Even among animals that have been brought under the dominion of man there is no trace of continuous intellectual advancement. Man takes advantage of some instinct implanted in them by nature, and contrives to modify it by long and careful training, so as to promote some object of his own; but, after all his labour, the original faculties and appetites of the animal are but little changed.

Unlike the lower orders of creatures, man comes into the world utterly ignorant of all that his fathers had learned before. His animal faculties and instincts exhibit in infancy a development far inferior to that which is found in other animals at a corresponding period of their being; but in a very brief space of time he excels them all in his intellectual acquirements, and manifests an aptitude for learning, and a desire for improvement, to which we can assign no limit, and which very clearly indicate a nobler nature and a higher destiny.

CONSCIENCE, OR THE MORAL SENSE.—This most important part of our rational constitution may be regarded as including both a faculty and an affection ; a faculty, by which we discriminate between the right and the wrong—and an affection, by which we are led to look on the one with approbation and pleasure, and on the other with condemnation and dislike. As very few subjects have given rise to so many conflicting opinions, we shall examine in order the more important propositions connected with it.

All men are conscious of a principle within them, by which they are enabled to determine between right and wrong. This is universally allowed to be the case, though wide differences of opinion exist in regard to its nature, and in reference to the standards by which its decisions are regulated. Even the hardened transgressor, who has habitually disregarded its claims, dares not deny its existence, and in the hours of calm reflection he is forced to acknowledge its power. Bishop Butler, who was the first that clearly pointed out the place and authority to which this principle is entitled, introduces his dissertation on the Nature of Virtue with the following observations, which are at once so clear and so ample as to leave no room for further remark :—

" Brute creatures are impressed and actuated by various instincts and propensities; so also are we. But in addition to this, we have a capacity of reflecting upon actions and characters, and of making them an object of thought. On doing this, we naturally and unavoidably approve some actions, under the peculiar view of their being virtuous and of good desert, and disapprove of others as vicious and of ill desert. That we have this moral approving and disapproving faculty is certain, from our experiencing it in ourselves, and recognising it in others. It appears from our exercising it unavoidably in the approbation and disapprobation even of feigned characters; from the words right and wrong, odious and amiable, base and worthy, with many others of like signification, in all languages, applied to actions and characters; from the many written systems of morals which suppose it, since it cannot be imagined that all these authors, throughout all these treatises, had absolutely no meaning to their words, or a meaning merely chimerical. It is manifest that a great part of common language, and of common behaviour over the world, is formed upon the supposition of such a moral faculty, whether it be called conscience, moral reason, moral sense, or divine reason; and whether it be considered as a sentiment of the understanding, or as a perception of the heart, or, which seems the truth, as including both."

It is universally agreed that this sense of right and wrong is the undoubted monarch of the sentiments and emotions, and that we are bound to give implicit obedience to its dictates, however unpalatable they may be. All men are conscious to themselves, that whatever the inward monitor points out as their duty, they cannot without shame and compunction neglect. They may debate the question, What is duty? But the place which duty is entitled to hold is intuitively perceived, and in all but the most hardened offenders is readily confessed.

A faculty so peculiar in its nature, and claiming for itself the supremacy over every other appetite and desire, naturally excites our attention, and leads us to inquire, What is the standard by which its decisions are regulated? The following is Bishop Butler's statement :—

" However much it may have been disputed, wherein virtue consists, and whatever ground for doubt there may be about particulars, yet in general there is in reality a universally acknowledged standard of it. It is that which all ages and all countries have made profession of in public; it is that which every man you meet puts on the show of; it is that which the primary and fundamental laws of civil constitutions over the earth make it their business and endeavour to enforce the practice upon mankind, namely, justice, veracity, and regard to the common good."

This statement is not sufficiently definite. " Justice, veracity, and regard to the common good," are not convertible terms. They express three very different and distinct ideas; and, if conscience has a varying standard, and directs our attention sometimes to one object, and sometimes to another, it cannot be fitted for the office which it claims. The subject is certainly one of some difficulty; but that difficulty will not be found very formidable, if we direct attention to the considerations by which conscience is regulated in its decisions. All will allow that they are those that involve *duty*, right, and obligation. In other words, they are those considerations which imply some present service that is *due* in consequence of a previously established relation. It is to this relationship that conscience, in the first place, directs its regard; and the consequences that may follow hold but a secondary place in the investigation. All the terms by which the performance of duty is expressed—such as honesty, honour, integrity, uprightness—distinctly imply the idea we have now set forth. Conscience decides on

principles precisely similar to those that direct a judge
on the bench. If a case is brought before a court of
justice, the decision is not determined by any regard
to the probable consequences that may arise, on the
one side or on the other, but by reference to the
agreement into which the parties have entered. In
like manner, conscience does not decide on future
contingencies, but on existing relations to our Creator,
to our families, and to our fellow-men, and on the
duties which these relations imply.

"It does not appear that brutes have any reflex sense of
actions, as distinguished from events, or that will and design,
which constitute the very nature of actions as such, are at all
an object of their perception. But to ours they are; and they
are the object, and the only one, of the approving and disapproving faculty."

Reason and conscience agree in this, that they
direct attention, not to the mere outward appearance
of the objects of which they take cognizance, but
to their original inherent properties and character.
Whether, therefore, we regard these mental attributes
as originally distinct, or look on them as modifications
of the same faculty, they stand so closely allied to
each other, and they differ in so many respects from
the inferior powers, that we can have no hesitation in
forming them into a class by themselves, and assigning to them a rank and an influence greatly superior
to the other faculties and feelings of our nature.
This supremacy is, in fact, acknowledged by all intelligent observers of the human constitution. We

must, therefore, regard the soul of man, of which they are the attributes, as essentially distinct in its nature, and greatly more exalted in its rank, than the spirit which animates the irrational creation.

MAN STANDS ALONE.

Amid all the vast variety of birds, and beasts, and creeping things that now inhabit the earth, man stands alone. His bodily organization, and his animal faculties, may be compared to those of other creatures, but the characteristic attributes of the soul are found only in him.

If we turn our attention to the ages of the past, and examine the organic remains of former times, we come to a similar conclusion. The records of geology are laid open to our view; we examine, one by one, their pages of stone, and they tell of unnumbered species and genera that have lived, and died, and been entombed; but from the earliest appearance of life on the globe, up to the day when man was formed, no trace can be found of any creature possessing intelligence like his. The era of the trilobite and mollusc, when animals of the lowest type were the chief inhabitants of earth, was followed by a period when the fishy tribes, of varied shape and monstrous size, became lords of the lower creation. The dynasty of the fish was succeeded by that of the saurian. The lizard monarchs of the water and the wood yielded in turn their supremacy to the mammal. But previous to the time when the human race appeared on the scene, during ages so long that they cannot be calculated, and among species and genera so numerous that their reckoning overwhelms us, there is no trace of any crea- ture endowed with the faculties and feelings of a rational mind, or entertaining the hopes and aspirations of an immortal soul. When man was created, a new element was introduced into the constitution of earthly things. Mineral, vegetable, and animal existences had been there before; but when he was brought into being, an intelligent and accountable creature became, for the first time, an inmate of the earth. His intro- duction into the terrestrial scene was the commence- ment of an era altogether new, of an epoch in creation higher and nobler than any that had gone before.

The transmutationists tell us that man differs from the lower creatures in degree of development, but not in essential nature. We maintain that the nature of man is altogether peculiar; that he is not to be classed or compared with any other inhabitant of earth; that he is as highly and as essentially exalted above the most intelligent of the irrational orders, as they are above the vegetable, and as the vegetable is above the stone. He stands alone, and his analogies are not to be sought for on earth, but in a higher sphere.

They point to bygone ages, and bid us look to the ape as the most distinguished of our ancestors, and to the snail as the founder of our family. We point to the future, and tell them of a destiny which eye hath not seen, nor ear heard, nor hath it entered into the heart of man to conceive. We tell them of an inheritance divine, of a progress onward and upward through the ages of eternity, when this mortal shall put on immortality, sharing the favour, and bearing the likeness of Him, who is God over all, blessed for evermore.

POSTSCRIPT.

THE author at one time intended to have concluded his review of Sir C. Lyell with some observations on the Mosaic narrative, in order to show how easily the record of Scripture may be reconciled with the discoveries of science. On further consideration, he has come to conclude that it is better the two subjects should be kept distinct; these observations, therefore, have been withheld.

While, however, he does not enter into any explanation of his views, or adduce any argument in support of them, he thinks it right to state the opinions which he has formed. He regards the submergence of the earth under the deep, spoken of in the first chapter of Genesis, as a simple literal fact. He believes that the creatures afterwards formed were cast, so to speak, in the same mould as those that had lived before; and that the present creation of irrational being is, in all its essential particulars, a restoration of that which previously existed. At the same time, he considers the events that accompanied the Adamic creation to have been of such a nature, that they left no evidence of their occurrence which can be perceived by geological research.

With this theory of interpretation, the idea of a

Pre-Adamite race of men, which has been advocated on various grounds, is in perfect accordance; and the remains of the human frame, and of works of art, found in the strata of the Post-pliocene period, might very naturally be regarded as the relics of those races which are now extinct.

Entertaining these views, the author does not object to Sir Charles's conclusions in regard to the antiquity of the earlier remains of man because they are contrary to Scripture; he rejects them simply because they are not supported by facts.

As to the speculations with respect to the origin of species and to the primeval condition of man, he does not see that they can by any possibility be reconciled with the narrative of inspiration; he, therefore, casts them aside as opposed alike to Scripture and to Science.

PRINTED BY CHARLES GIBSON, THISTLE STREET, EDINBURGH.